Mary Engelbreit's

Queen of the Kitchen

cookbook

Mary Engelbreit's
Queen of the Kitchen
cookbook

Illustrated by Mary Engelbreit

Photographs by Alison Miksch

Andrews McMeel
Publishing

Kansas City

www.maryengelbreit.com

 is a registered trademark of Mary Engelbreit Enterprises, Inc.

Library of Congress Cataloging-in-Publication Data as Cataloged for the Hardcover Edition

Engelbreit, Mary.

    Mary Engelbreit's queen of the kitchen cookbook / illustrated by Mary Engelbreit.

        p. cm.

    Includes index.

    ISBN 0-7407-4146-2 (paperback)

        1. Cookery. 2. Menus. I. Andrews McMeel

    TX7140.Q44 1998

    641.5—dc21   98-22459
                                                                 CIP

04 05 06 07 08 MON 10 9 8 7 6 5 4 3 2 1

Editor: Deborah Mintcheff
Designer: Nina Ovryn
Photographer: Alison Miksch
Food Stylist: William Smith
Prop Stylist: Barbara Fritz

Produced by Smallwood & Stewart, Inc., New York City

ATTENTION: SCHOOLS AND BUSINESSES

Andrews McMeel books are available at quantity discounts with bulk purchase for educational, business, or sales promotional use.

For information, please write to: Special Sales Department, Andrews McMeel Publishing, 4520 Main Street, Kansas City, Missouri 64111.

table of Contents

Introduction

do you dream of being the queen of your kitchen? I certainly imagine what it would be like if I had the time to devote to cooking and entertaining. But as the head chef at Mary Engelbreit Studios (and editor in chief of a magazine), my busy schedule doesn't allow it. I'm constantly rearranging my schedule in order to keep sacred the time I do have with my family. A reporter once asked me if I could cook. I answered her honestly: If my family had to depend on me for food they would starve to death in a really cute kitchen. But let me point out that my husband, Phil, is a terrific chef, and our family doesn't subsist on fast food or TV dinners. In fact, it's quite the opposite! Even though I do not devote my time to cooking, I still love and appreciate good food. In this book I can share with you some of the food I love. It contains wonderful recipes, developed by cooking experts, and it's designed to make it easy for busy cooks to get back in charge of the kitchen with a minimum of fuss. There is nothing more nurturing to family and friends than a meal that is lovingly prepared and presented. I hope that this book will help you put together fantastic meals and menus that your family and friends love, and I sincerely hope that your family will show their appreciation to the cook by helping to clean up the kitchen afterward.

Good luck!

Mary

Chapter One

Appetizers

flaky cheddar *Biscuits*

t hese foolproof savory snacks are ideal party food. Bake them in advance, freeze, and when needed, reheat in a 350°F oven for about 10 minutes, or until warmed through. They make delicious little sandwiches when split, spread lightly with chutney butter, and filled with paper-thin slices of ham or smoked turkey.

3/4 cup plus 2 tablespoons all-purpose flour

2 teaspoons baking powder

1/4 teaspoon baking soda

1/4 teaspoon salt

1/2 cup grated cheddar cheese

2 tablespoons vegetable shortening, chilled

1/4 cup Spanish-style pimiento-stuffed green olives, finely chopped

1/4 cup plus 2 tablespoons buttermilk or plain yogurt

1. Preheat the oven to 450°F.

2. Into a medium bowl, sift together the flour, baking powder, baking soda, and salt. Using a pastry blender or two forks, cut the cheese and shortening into the flour until the mixture resembles coarse crumbs. Stir in the olives.

3. Make a well in the center of the flour mixture and pour in the buttermilk. With a fork, gently toss until the mixture is just moistened; do not overmix. (The dough will be sticky.)

4. Turn the dough out onto a well-floured surface and knead once or twice with floured hands, sprinkling the dough lightly with flour. Pat the dough to a 1/2-inch thickness.

5. Dip a 1 1/2-inch biscuit cutter into flour and cut out biscuits, pushing the cutter straight down into the dough and pulling it out without twisting. Arrange the biscuits about 1 inch apart on an ungreased baking sheet. Re-roll the scraps.

6. Bake for 12 to 15 minutes, until golden. Serve warm.

MAKES ABOUT 2 DOZEN

appetizers

lemon-parmesan Wafers

Warm from the oven, these make a light and lovely hors d'oeuvre when served with chilled rosé or white wine. Prepare the dough up to several hours ahead.

1 1/2 cups freshly grated Parmesan
   cheese (6 ounces)

3/4 cup all-purpose flour

1 teaspoon grated lemon zest

1/2 teaspoon ground coriander

1 teaspoon coarsely ground pepper

1/4 cup (1/2 stick) cold unsalted butter,
   cut into pieces

1 1/2 tablespoons ice-cold water

1 teaspoon fresh lemon juice

1. In a medium bowl, whisk together the Parmesan, flour, lemon zest, coriander, and pepper. Using a pastry blender, cut in the butter until the mixture resembles coarse crumbs. Sprinkle the water and lemon juice over the flour and toss lightly with a fork just until the dough comes together.

2. On a lightly floured work surface, knead the dough several times, then transfer to a sheet of waxed paper. Shape into an 11 x 1 1/2-inch square-sided loaf. Wrap the dough in the waxed paper and chill for at least 1 hour, or until firm.

3. Preheat the oven to 375°F.

4. Cut the dough into 1/4-inch slices and arrange 1 inch apart on ungreased baking sheets. Bake for 12 to 15 minutes, until deep golden around the edges. Transfer to wire racks. Serve warm.

MAKES ABOUT 4 DOZEN

savory stuffed Mushrooms

these bite-size morsels are perfect with chilled white wine. Don't be concerned if you're not crazy about anchovies. You will hardly know they are there.

24 small white mushrooms

1/2 cup fresh bread crumbs

3 tablespoons freshly grated Parmesan cheese

1 tablespoon finely chopped fresh flat-leaf parsley plus 24 small leaves for garnish

4 anchovy fillets, drained, rinsed, and mashed to a paste

2 to 3 tablespoons fruity olive oil

1 tablespoon red wine vinegar, or to taste

Salt and freshly ground pepper

1. Preheat the oven to 350°F.

2. Remove the mushroom stems and mince them. Place the mushroom caps upside down on a baking sheet and set aside.

3. In a medium bowl, mix the minced stems, bread crumbs, Parmesan, parsley, anchovies, oil, and vinegar. Season with salt and pepper. Stuff each mushroom cap, mounding them slightly.

4. Bake the mushrooms for 15 minutes, or until just tender. Arrange them on a serving plate, garnish each with a parsley leaf, and serve. **SERVES 8**

fresh tomato Salsa

appetizers

Once you've tried this quick-to-prepare salsa made with ripe red tomatoes, you won't settle for the mushy supermarket variety. Make a big batch of salsa and serve with roasted chicken, dollop onto hamburgers, or spoon over steamed green beans or asparagus. Or enjoy it in traditional Southwestern style—with a bowl of crisp tortilla chips and a pitcher of ice-cold margaritas.

1 tablespoon ground cumin

3 large tomatoes (about 1 1/2 pounds), cut into large chunks

1/3 cup chopped fresh cilantro, including some stems

1/3 cup chopped onion

1 to 2 tablespoons seeded and finely chopped pickled jalapeño peppers

2 tablespoons fresh lime juice

Salt

1. In a small heavy or nonstick skillet, toast the cumin over medium-high heat, stirring frequently, for about 3 minutes, or until the cumin is fragrant and the color has darkened. Transfer the cumin to a medium bowl.

2. In a food processor, chop the tomatoes, in batches, and add to the cumin. Add the cilantro, onion, jalapeños, lime juice, and 3/4 teaspoon salt and toss until combined. Cover the salsa and let stand at room temperature for 30 minutes to blend the flavors.

MAKES 3 CUPS

chunky Guacamole

t here are probably as many incarnations of this classic Mexican dip as people who love to eat it. Fragrant cilantro, aromatic cumin, and vibrant jalapeños make this version a favorite. Guacamole tastes best when it's fresh, but if you prefer to make it in advance, press plastic wrap directly onto the surface and refrigerate for up to several hours; serve at room temperature for the most flavor.

2 ripe Hass avocados, halved, pitted, and peeled

1 cup diced (1/4-inch) tomatoes

1/3 cup finely chopped onion, such as Vidalia

1/3 cup coarsely chopped fresh cilantro

1 to 2 teaspoons seeded and minced

    jalapeño peppers

2 tablespoons fresh lime juice

1/2 teaspoon ground cumin

Salt

A few drops of hot red pepper sauce, or to taste

1. In a medium bowl, coarsely mash the avocados.

2. Add the tomatoes, onion, cilantro, jalapeño, lime juice, cumin, 1/2 teaspoon salt, and hot pepper sauce. Toss until mixed. Spoon into a bowl and serve.

MAKES 2 1/4 CUPS

sweet & Spicy nuts

t his is a great make-ahead snack. Prepare the nuts in large batches, transfer to containers, and freeze for up to several months. When friends drop by, simply thaw and serve, or recrisp in a 300°F oven.

1 large egg white

3/4 cup sugar

1 tablespoon chili powder

1 1/2 teaspoons ground cumin

1/2 teaspoon ground cinnamon

Salt

1/8 teaspoon ground red pepper

2 cups mixed nuts, such as pecans, almonds,

    and/or cashews

1. Preheat the oven to 325°F. Spray 2 jelly-roll pans or baking sheets with nonstick cooking spray.

2. In a medium bowl, whisk the egg white until frothy. In a pie plate, mix the sugar, chili powder, cumin, cinnamon, 1/2 teaspoon salt, and ground red pepper.

3. Working in small batches and using a slotted spoon, toss the nuts in the egg white. Lift the nuts onto the spoon, letting the excess drip off. Toss the nuts in the spiced mixture, tossing until coated. Spread the nuts in a single layer in the prepared pans.

4. Bake for 15 minutes, or until the nuts are crisp and the coating is lightly browned. Let cool in the pans, then loosen the nuts with a spatula and transfer to a serving dish.

MAKES 2 CUPS

gravlax with Mustard sauce

gravlax is a popular Swedish specialty. The salmon is served in paper-thin slices and accompanied by mustard sauce and black bread. For special occasions, gravlax is an elegant choice: It's utterly delicious and surprisingly easy to prepare. Make it two days before you're ready to entertain—the gravlax will be marinated to perfection.

> One 2-pound salmon fillet, skin left on
>
> 3 tablespoons plus 1 teaspoon sugar
>
> 3 tablespoons Kosher salt
>
> 1 tablespoon cracked white pepper
>
> 1 tablespoon cracked black pepper
>
> 1 bunch fresh dill, tough stems removed
>
> 1/2 cup grainy mustard
>
> 2 teaspoons cider vinegar
>
> Black bread, for serving

1. Trim any excess fat from the salmon and, with tweezers or small clean pliers, remove any small bones. Cut the fillet crosswise in half and place one piece skin side down in a 9-inch square baking dish. Set the second piece aside.

2. In a small bowl, mix 3 tablespoons of the sugar, the salt, and the white and black pepper. Sprinkle half of the mixture over the salmon. Finely chop enough of the dill to equal 1 tablespoon and set aside. Reserve a few dill sprigs for garnish and cover the salmon with the remaining sprigs. Place the second piece of salmon skin side up on top. Sprinkle the remaining sugar mixture over the salmon.

3. Cover the salmon with plastic wrap and place a piece of cardboard, cut slightly smaller than the baking dish, on top. Place a 5-pound weight (such as several cans) on the cardboard and refrigerate for 48 hours, turning the salmon over several times while it marinates.

4. Meanwhile, make the mustard sauce: In a small bowl, stir together the mustard, the chopped dill, the vinegar, and the remaining 1 teaspoon sugar. Refrigerate.

5. To serve the gravlax, remove the salmon from the dish and scrape off the dill and most of the pepper. Using a long thin knife, cut the gravlax into very thin slices and arrange on a serving platter. Garnish with the reserved dill sprigs and serve accompanied by the mustard sauce and black bread.

SERVES 10 TO 12

Cocktail Party

Gravlax with Mustard Sauce

Savory Stuffed Mushrooms
page 12

Roasted Tomatoes with Brie
page 16

Lemon-Parmesan Wafers
page 11

Sweet and Spicy Nuts
page 13

roasted tomatoes with *Brie*

t he marriage of oven-roasted tomatoes, ripe Brie cheese, and pungent pesto is a happy one. Roast the tomatoes in the morning, then cover and set aside at room temperature until ready to serve. It will take only a few minutes to compose the finished hors d'oeuvres.

10 medium plum tomatoes

Salt and freshly ground pepper

2 teaspoons olive oil, preferably
    extra-virgin

About 1 tablespoon pesto
    (store-bought or homemade)

4 ounces ripe Brie cheese,
    cut into 20 thin slices

20 small fresh flat-leaf parsley or
    basil leaves, for garnish (optional)

appetizers

1. Preheat the oven to 325°F. Lightly oil a jelly-roll pan.

2. Cut the tomatoes lengthwise in half and scoop out the seeds with the tip of a teaspoon or a melon baller, leaving the membranes intact. Arrange the tomatoes cut-side up in the prepared pan. Sprinkle with 1/4 teaspoon salt, 1/8 teaspoon pepper, and drizzle with the oil.

3. Roast the tomatoes for about 50 minutes, or until they are very soft. Let the tomatoes rest until warm, then arrange them on a small platter.

4. Spoon a dab of pesto onto each tomato half and top with a slice of Brie. Decorate each with a parsley leaf, if using, and serve immediately.

SERVES 6 TO 8

tapenade *Pinwheels*

f rozen puff pastry is especially good to keep on hand, and it makes this savory appetizer very simple to prepare. If desired, wrap the unsliced rolls tightly in foil and freeze for up to a month. An hour before serving, thaw at room temperature, then slice and bake as directed.

TAPENADE

1/3 cup pimiento-stuffed green olives, rinsed, drained, and patted dry

1/3 cup pitted ripe black olives, rinsed, drained, and patted dry

2 garlic cloves, crushed through a press

2 tablespoons unsalted butter, at room temperature

1 sheet frozen puff pastry (half of a 17 1/4-ounce box), thawed according to package directions

1 egg, lightly beaten

1 tablespoon plus 1 teaspoon unsalted butter, melted

1. In a food processor, combine the green and black olives and the garlic and pulse until very finely chopped but not pureed. Add the butter and pulse just until blended. Set aside.

2. On a lightly floured work surface, with a floured rolling pin, roll the pastry sheet to a 14- x 11-inch rectangle. Brush off the excess flour from both sides of the pastry and trim the edges even. Leaving a 1 1/2-inch border along one of the long sides and a 1/2-inch border along the other three sides, spread the filling evenly over the pastry.

3. Lightly brush the 1 1/2-inch border with the beaten egg. Starting from the opposite side, roll up the pastry jelly-roll style. Place seam-side down on a baking sheet and freeze for at least 1 hour, or until very firm.

4. Preheat the oven to 400°F. Grease two jelly-roll pans.

5. Remove the pastry from the freezer. With a sharp knife, cut the roll into 1/2-inch slices and arrange 2 inches apart in the prepared pans. Lightly brush the slices with the melted butter. Place a baking sheet under each jelly-roll pan to prevent the pastries from burning on the bottom.

6. Bake for 10 minutes, or until the pastries are golden brown on the bottom. Turn over and bake for 7 to 10 minutes longer, until the second side is golden brown and crisp. Immediately transfer the pastries to wire racks and let cool slightly. Arrange on a platter and serve.

MAKES ABOUT 2 DOZEN

buffalo chicken Wings

b roiling makes these wings wonderfully crisp without the fat and fuss of deep-frying. Serve this favorite finger food accompanied by one of the new hot pepper sauces, so readily available in supermarkets, that offers the flavor of different chiles.

2 pounds chicken wings, wing tips cut off
and cut apart at the second joint
Salt
2 tablespoons butter
1 tablespoon white wine vinegar
Hot red pepper sauce to taste
Celery sticks, for serving

appetizers

1. Preheat the broiler.

2. Season the chicken wings with 1/2 teaspoon salt and arrange on the rack of the broiler pan. Broil 4 to 6 inches from the heat for 10 minutes. Turn the wings and broil for 8 to 10 minutes longer, until deep golden brown and cooked through, watching to make sure the wings don't burn.

3. Meanwhile, in a small saucepan, melt the butter over low heat. Remove from the heat and stir in the vinegar and hot pepper sauce. Cover to keep warm.

4. With tongs, transfer the wings to paper towel–lined plates. Drain briefly, then transfer to a large bowl and toss with the butter sauce until well coated.

5. Arrange the wings on a small platter and serve along with the celery sticks and the Blue Cheese Dressing.

S E R V E S   4   T O   6

BLUE CHEESE DRESSING

1/2 cup sour cream
1/4 cup mayonnaise
1/4 cup crumbled blue cheese
1 tablespoon vinegar
Salt and freshly ground pepper
2 tablespoons chopped fresh parsley

In a blender or food processor, combine the sour cream, mayonnaise, blue cheese, vinegar, and salt and pepper to taste. Process until smooth. Transfer to a bowl and stir in the parsley.

Superbowl Party

Buffalo Chicken Wings

Fresh Tomato Salsa and Chips
page 12

Mixed Green Salad
Honey-Mustard Dressing
page 100

Chunky Beef Chili
page 54

Monterey Jack
and Jalapeño Cornbread
page 98

Chapter Two

Soups

roasted red Pepper soup

u sing too many canned products at one time often gives food a "tinny" taste. In this pantry soup, the flavors of canned tomatoes, chicken broth, and roasted red peppers are accentuated with the addition of Pernod and thyme. Crowned with a zesty lemon-scented sour cream topping, this soup makes a worthy first course, especially during the holidays. It's also delicious cold: simply substitute three tablespoons of olive oil for the butter.

1/4 cup (1/2 stick) butter

4 medium onions, finely chopped

2 garlic cloves, minced

2 (14-ounce) cans whole tomatoes,
    undrained

1 cup canned crushed tomatoes

2 (13 3/4- to 14 1/2-ounce) cans
    low-sodium chicken broth

2 (7-ounce) jars roasted red peppers,
    drained and chopped

1 tablespoon Pernod or other anise-flavored
    liqueur (optional)

2 teaspoons fresh thyme leaves, plus 8 sprigs
    for garnish or 3/4 teaspoon dried

Salt and freshly ground pepper

1/2 cup sour cream

1 teaspoon grated lemon zest

1. In a large nonreactive pot, melt the butter over medium heat. Add the onions and cook, stirring occasionally, for 5 minutes, or until softened. Add the garlic and cook, stirring, for 2 minutes longer. Add the whole tomatoes and their juice, the crushed tomatoes, and broth and simmer for 5 minutes. Add the roasted peppers, the Pernod if using, and the thyme and simmer for 5 minutes longer.

2. In a blender or food processor, process the soup until pureed, working in batches if necessary. Pour the soup through a strainer set over a large bowl, pressing on the solids with the back of a wooden spoon to extract as much of the liquid as possible; discard the solids.

3. Return the soup to the same cleaned-out pot, season with salt and pepper, and bring to a simmer over medium heat.

4. Meanwhile, in a small bowl, stir together the sour cream and lemon zest.

5. To serve, ladle the hot soup into small deep bowls and top with a dollop of the lemon sour cream. Garnish with the fresh thyme if using. **S E R V E S   8**

wild mushroom & Barley soup

t he deep, woodsy flavor of this mushroom-laden soup will warm you up, right down to your toes. Serve with thickly sliced whole-grain bread, a cherry tomato salad, and a generous wedge of sharp cheddar cheese. Double the recipe and freeze a batch so you'll have soup on hand whenever you need some comfort food.

1/3 cup medium pearl barley

4 cups canned low-sodium chicken broth

1 cup water

1/4 cup dried mushrooms

3 tablespoons extra-virgin olive oil

1 large onion, finely chopped

2 garlic cloves, minced

1/2 teaspoon dried thyme, crumbled

1/4 teaspoon dried rosemary, crumbled

3/4 pound white mushrooms, sliced

1/2 pound assorted wild mushrooms, such
   as creminis and shiitakes, sliced, shiitake
   stems discarded

Salt and freshly ground pepper

1/4 cup chopped fresh dill or parsley

soups

1. In a medium saucepan, put the barley, 1 cup of the chicken broth, and the water. Cover and bring to a boil over high heat. Reduce the heat to low, cover, and simmer for 30 to 40 minutes, until the barley is tender. Remove from the heat.

2. Meanwhile, in a small saucepan, bring 1 cup water to a boil. Remove from the heat, stir in the dried mushrooms, and let stand for 10 to 20 minutes, until the mushrooms are softened.

3. Using a slotted spoon, remove the mushrooms and coarsely chop them. Pour the mushroom liquid through a paper towel–lined strainer set over a small bowl. Set the mushrooms and the mushroom liquid aside.

4. In a Dutch oven, heat the oil over medium heat. Add the onion, garlic, thyme, and rosemary and cook, stirring, for about 4 minutes, or until the onion is softened. Increase the heat to high and add the fresh mushrooms. Sprinkle with 1/4 teaspoon salt, season with pepper, and toss to mix. Cook, stirring, for 5 to 6 minutes, until the mushrooms are tender and beginning to give up their liquid. Add the dried mushrooms and cook, stirring, for 2 minutes longer.

5. Add the barley and any cooking liquid, the remaining broth, and the dried mushroom liquid to the pot and bring to a boil. Reduce the heat to low, partially cover, and simmer for 10 minutes. Stir in the dill and serve.

S E R V E S   6

weeknight bean & *Bacon* soup

C anadian bacon keeps the flavor high and the calories low in this hearty soup. You'll find that it freezes well—even the parsley stays green! Serve with a crisp salad and some grilled cheese-and-tomato sandwiches for a satisfying, casual meal.

2 tablespoons extra-virgin olive oil

1 large onion, chopped

2 medium celery stalks, chopped

2 garlic cloves, minced

3 ounces sliced Canadian bacon, cut into

1/4-inch pieces

1 teaspoon chopped fresh rosemary or

1/4 teaspoon dried

2 (15-ounce) cans small white beans, such as

Great Northern or navy, drained and rinsed

1 large baking potato (about 12 ounces),

peeled and cut into chunks

4 cups canned low-sodium chicken broth

Freshly ground pepper

1/4 cup chopped fresh parsley

1. In a large pot, heat the oil over medium heat. Add the onion, celery, and garlic and cook, stirring, for 6 minutes, or until the vegetables are softened.

2. Add the Canadian bacon and rosemary and cook, stirring,

for 1 minute. Stir in the beans, potato, broth, and 1/4 teaspoon pepper and bring to a boil over high heat. Reduce the heat to medium-low. Cover and simmer, stirring occasionally, for 15 minutes, or until the potato is very tender.

3. With a potato masher, coarsely mash the beans and potato. Stir in the parsley and serve.

S E R V E S 4 T O 5

Kitchen Soup Party

Tomato and
Red Onion Salad

Spicy Tomato Vinaigrette
page 101

Weeknight Bean
& Bacon Soup

Hearty Chicken
and Sausage Gumbo
page 25

Basket of Warm Breads

Herbed Butters

Pineapple
Upside-Down Cake
page 115

23

soups

hearty chicken & sausage *Gumbo*

 classic of Cajun cooking, gumbo is the name given to any thick soup or stew from southern Louisiana prepared with a dark brown roux (a mixture of flour and fat) and thickened with okra or filé powder. Filé powder, made from the ground dried leaves of the sassafras tree, is used here. It is available in specialty food stores.

4 chicken thighs (about 1 1/4 pounds)

2 celery stalks with leaves, chopped

4 garlic cloves, halved

1 bay leaf

4 cups water

Salt

1/4 cup vegetable oil

1/4 cup (1/2 stick) butter

1/2 cup all-purpose flour

1 large red onion, chopped

1 yellow bell pepper, cored,
    seeded, and chopped

1/2 pound andouille or other
    spicy smoked sausage, cut into
    1/4-inch slices

1/2 teaspoon filé powder

Freshly ground pepper

1/2 cup finely chopped scallions

1/2 cup finely chopped fresh parsley

Hot cooked rice, for serving

1. In a Dutch oven, combine the chicken, celery, garlic, bay leaf, water, and salt to taste and bring to a boil over high heat. Reduce the heat and simmer, covered, for 30 minutes, or until the chicken is cooked through.

2. With a slotted spoon, transfer the chicken to a plate and discard the bay leaf. Set the pot with the broth aside. When the chicken is cool enough to handle, finely shred the meat, discarding the skin and bones.

3. Meanwhile, in a large heavy skillet, heat the oil and butter over medium heat until very hot but not smoking. Whisk in the flour and cook, whisking constantly, for 10 minutes, or until the mixture turns dark golden brown (the color of peanut butter). Add the onion, bell pepper, sausage, filé powder, and 1/2 teaspoon or more pepper and cook, stirring, for 2 minutes.

4. Stir the vegetable mixture into the broth, bring to a simmer, and simmer, uncovered, stirring occasionally, for 40 minutes, or until the vegetables are tender and the flavor is very rich.

5. Season the gumbo with salt and pepper if needed. Add the chicken, scallions, and all but 1 tablespoon of the parsley to the pot and simmer for 5 minutes, or until the gumbo is heated through.

6. Ladle the gumbo into bowls, sprinkle with the remaining 1 tablespoon parsley, and serve accompanied by rice.

SERVES 4

quick Gazpacho

soups

this easy-to-make soup is delicious and refreshing during warm weather when no one wants to spend a lot of time in the kitchen. For the most appealing texture, chop the tomato a bit coarser than the cucumber, onion, and pepper. This will give the soup its classic chunkiness. And for a professional-looking finish, garnish each serving with additional vegetables that are finely chopped by hand. To keep the gazpacho cold when served, chill the soup bowls.

1 garlic clove

1 1/2 cups tomato juice

3 large tomatoes (about 1 1/2 pounds),
   cut into large chunks

1 large red bell pepper, cored and
   cut into large chunks

1/2 large green bell pepper, cut
   into large chunks

1 large cucumber, peeled, halved
   lengthwise, seeded, and cut
   into large chunks

1/2 large red onion, cut into chunks

3 tablespoons extra-virgin olive oil

3 tablespoons red wine vinegar

Salt and freshly ground pepper

1/8 teaspoon ground red pepper

Finely chopped red and green bell peppers,
   cucumber, and onion, for garnish

1. In a food processor with the motor running, drop the garlic and a little of the tomato juice through the feed tube and process until the garlic is finely chopped. Add the tomatoes and a little tomato juice in batches and process, pulsing just until the tomatoes are chopped. Transfer the mixture to a large bowl. Process the bell peppers, cucumber, and onion in batches until chopped, then add to the tomatoes.

2. Add the remaining tomato juice, the oil, vinegar, 3/4 teaspoon salt, 1/4 teaspoon pepper, and the ground red pepper and stir to mix. Cover and refrigerate for at least 2 hours, until very cold. To serve, ladle the chilled soup into bowls and garnish with chopped vegetables.

SERVES 5 TO 6

Summer Supper

Crisp Cornmeal-Fried Tomatoes
page 95

Shrimp with Creole Sauce
page 71

Hot White Rice

Monterey Jack
and Jalapeño Cornbread
page 98

Blueberry Sorbet with
Melon Ribbons
page 141

summer Tomato-basil soup

basil and tomato are the ultimate summer flavors, and this light soup takes advantage of both. Make it when tomatoes are at their flavorful best—the better the tomatoes, the better the soup. For a refreshing alternative, serve the soup chilled. And for a taste of summer during the wintertime, leave out the basil and freeze for up to several months. Thaw, reheat, and swirl in a little black-olive puree just before serving.

- 1 tablespoon fruity olive oil
- 1 celery stalk with leaves, chopped
- 1 carrot, finely chopped
- 3 large shallots, chopped
- 6 fresh parsley sprigs
- 1 garlic clove, minced
- 4 pounds ripe tomatoes (about 10 medium), chopped
- 1 (14 1/2-ounce) can vegetable or chicken broth
- 1/2 cup water
- Salt and freshly ground pepper
- 1/4 cup finely shredded fresh basil leaves, for garnish

1. In a large nonreactive pot, heat the oil over low heat. Add the celery, carrot, and shallots, and cook, stirring, for 10 minutes, or until the celery and shallots are softened. Add the parsley sprigs and garlic and cook for 1 minute. Add the tomatoes, broth, water, 3/4 teaspoon salt, and 1/4 teaspoon pepper and bring to a boil over high heat. Reduce the heat to medium-low and cook for 45 minutes, or until thickened.

2. In a food processor or blender, process the soup until smooth, working in batches if necessary. Pour the soup through a strainer set over a large bowl, pressing on the solids with the back of a wooden spoon to extract all the liquid; discard the solids.

3. Return the soup to the cleaned-out pot and bring to a simmer over medium heat. To serve, ladle the soup into bowls and garnish with the basil. **SERVES 6**

soups

chunky vegetable *Soup* with pesto

 Welcome spring with this fresh-tasting vegetable soup. It has its roots in the French soup *garbure* (very similar to minestrone), which is traditionally served with *pistou*, French "pesto." If fresh tomatoes are in season, you may want to use them, but make sure to peel them first. Accompany the soup with bread toasts sprinkled with grated Parmesan cheese and broiled until nice and melted.

3 tablespoons extra-virgin olive oil

1 large onion, halved and thinly sliced

4 garlic cloves, minced

1/2 teaspoon dried sage, crumbled

1/2 teaspoon dried marjoram, crumbled

Salt and freshly ground pepper

3 large carrots, thinly sliced

1/2 pound red-skinned potatoes, cut
   into 1-inch chunks

2 (14 1/2-ounce) cans vegetable or
   low-sodium chicken broth

3 cups water

3 cups coarsely chopped green cabbage

1 (28-ounce) can whole tomatoes,
   drained and coarsely chopped

1 medium summer squash, halved
   lengthwise and cut into
   1/4-inch slices

1/2 cup frozen petite peas

**About 3 tablespoons pesto (store-bought
or homemade)**

1. In a large nonreactive pot, heat the oil over medium heat. Add the onion, garlic, sage, marjoram, 1/2 teaspoon salt, and 1/4 teaspoon pepper and cook, stirring, for 4 to 5 minutes, until the onion is softened. Add the carrots, reduce the heat to medium-low, and cook, stirring, for about 4 minutes, or until they just begin to soften.

2. Add the potatoes, broth, and water. Cover and bring to a boil. Reduce the heat to low and simmer for 10 minutes. Stir in the cabbage and tomatoes, return the soup to a simmer, and cook for 15 minutes. Stir in the squash and peas and simmer for about 8 minutes longer, or until all the vegetables are tender.

3. To serve, ladle the soup into bowls and top each serving with a small dollop of the pesto.

S E R V E S   8

29

smoky shrimp & Corn chowder

i t's best to make this crowd-pleasing chowder during the summer, when corn, tomatoes, and basil are at their peak of flavor. Served with buttermilk biscuits, a green salad, and Fresh Nectarine and Blueberry Cobbler (page 131), this is the epitome of great summertime food.

4 slices bacon, cut into

   1/2-inch strips

3 small red onions, cut into 1/4-inch dice

1 jalapeño pepper, seeded, ribs removed,

   and minced

2 tablespoons all-purpose flour

1 garlic clove, minced

Salt and freshly ground pepper

3 (14 1/2-ounce) cans low-sodium

   chicken broth

1 pound red-skinned potatoes, cut into

   1/2-inch cubes

1 pound small shrimp,

   shelled and deveined

2 cups fresh, thawed frozen,

   or drained canned corn kernels

1/3 cup heavy cream

2 plum tomatoes, seeded and cut into

   1/2-inch chunks, for garnish

8 small fresh basil leaves, for garnish

soups

1. In a Dutch oven, cook the bacon over medium heat until crisp and browned. With a slotted spoon, transfer the bacon to a paper towel–lined plate.

2. Add the onions and jalapeño to the pot and cook, stirring, for 5 minutes, or until softened. Stir in the flour and garlic, season with salt and pepper, and cook, stirring, for 2 minutes longer. Add the broth and bring to a boil. Add the potatoes, reduce the heat, and simmer for 10 to 15 minutes, until the potatoes are tender when pierced with a fork.

3. Add the shrimp, corn, and cream and cook for about 3 minutes, or until the shrimp are just cooked through. Remove from the heat.

4. Meanwhile, finely shred the basil leaves.

5. To serve, transfer the soup to a tureen and garnish with the bacon, tomato, and basil. **SERVES 8**

Chapter Three

MainCourses

rosemary-roasted Chicken

everyone has an opinion about how to achieve a perfectly roasted chicken—one with crisp, golden brown skin and juicy, flavorful meat. We think this is the best recipe yet. The chicken is slowly roasted at a moderate temperature and basted occasionally, which keeps the meat moist and helps the skin get nice and crispy. The juice of one lemon, squeezed over the chicken, brightens the flavor and complements the generous dose of fresh rosemary.

main courses

1 (5 1/2- to 6-pound) chicken

Salt and freshly ground pepper

1 1/2 small lemons

6 garlic cloves, unpeeled

1 tablespoon chopped fresh rosemary plus
   sprigs for garnish, or 2 teaspoons dried

2 tablespoons extra-virgin olive oil

Lemon wedges, for garnish

PAN GRAVY

1 1/2 cups canned low-sodium chicken broth

2 tablespoons water blended with
   1 tablespoon plus 1 teaspoon
   all-purpose flour

Salt and freshly ground pepper

Fresh lemon juice to taste
   (optional)

1. Preheat the oven to 425°F.

2. Rinse the chicken inside and out and pat dry. Season the chicken with 1 teaspoon salt and 1/2 teaspoon pepper. Tuck the wings under and place the chicken on a rack in a roasting pan. Squeeze the juice of 1 lemon over the skin and in the cavity of the chicken. Put the garlic cloves into the cavity and tie the legs together.

3. Cut the remaining lemon half into four pieces and place around the chicken. Sprinkle the rosemary over the chicken, then drizzle the oil over it.

4. Roast for 30 minutes. Reduce the oven temperature to 350°F and roast, basting occasionally, for 1 1/2 to 2 hours longer, until an instant-read thermometer inserted in the thickest part of the thigh (not touching the bone) registers 180°F. Transfer the chicken to a plate, garnish with rosemary sprigs and lemon wedges, cover loosely with foil, and set aside.

5. Discard the roasted lemon pieces. Skim off and discard the fat from the pan juices and pour the juices into a medium saucepan. Pour the broth into the roasting pan and heat over medium heat, scraping with a wooden spoon to loosen the browned bits in the bottom of the pan. Pour through a strainer set over the saucepan.

6. Put the saucepan over medium heat and gradually add the flour mixture, whisking constantly. Continue whisking until the gravy thickens and boils. Reduce the heat to medium-low and simmer for 3 minutes. Stir in any accumulated chicken juices, season with salt and pepper if needed, and add some lemon juice, if desired.

7. Serve the chicken accompanied by the gravy.

S E R V E S   6   T O   8

citrus-grilled Cornish hens

there is something special about being served a whole game hen. Cornish hens, more deeply flavored than chicken, are a good match for the assertive tropical blend in this marinade. If you prefer more heat, sprinkle in some extra red pepper flakes.

4 Cornish game hens

    (1- to 1 1/4-pounds each)

1 cup orange juice

1/4 cup fresh lime juice

2 tablespoons extra-virgin olive oil

1/3 cup coarsely chopped fresh cilantro,

    plus whole sprigs for garnish

3 garlic cloves, minced

2 teaspoons ground cumin

Salt

1/2 teaspoon crushed red pepper flakes

Orange sections and lime wedges,

    for garnish

1. With poultry shears, cut off the wing tips from the hens. Cut down along both sides of each backbone to remove it and discard. Lay the hens out flat, skin side up, and press down firmly to flatten. Put into a large shallow baking dish.

2. In a medium bowl, whisk together the orange and lime juices, the oil, cilantro, garlic, cumin, 1 teaspoon salt, and the red pepper flakes. Pour the marinade over the hens, turning to coat well. Cover and marinate at least 8 hours or overnight, turning the hens once or twice.

3. Preheat the grill to medium. Pour the marinade into a saucepan, bring to a rolling boil, and boil for 1 full minute.

4. Oil the grill. Place the hens, skin side down, on the grill and brush generously with the marinade. Cover and grill, basting several times, for about 15 minutes, or until the skin is browned. Turn the hens over and grill, basting, for about 10 minutes longer, or until browned and cooked through.

5. Transfer the hens to a platter. Garnish with cilantro sprigs, orange sections, and lime wedges, and serve.

S E R V E S   4

main courses

crispy mustard Chicken

t his is a great party dish. The chicken can be prepared up to several hours ahead and baked just before guests arrive. While the chicken bakes in the oven, you can make the mustard-cream sauce—a delicately piquant blend of grainy mustard, mushrooms, cream, and flavorful pan juices.

1/4 cup grainy mustard

2 teaspoons Dijon mustard

1/2 cup fine dried bread crumbs

Salt and freshly ground pepper

6 skinless boneless chicken breast halves

(about 5 ounces each)

About 2 tablespoons olive oil

2 tablespoons unsalted butter

10 ounces small white mushrooms, sliced

(about 3 cups)

4 scallions, thinly sliced

3/4 cup dry white wine

3/4 cup chicken broth

3/4 cup heavy cream

Fresh lemon juice to taste

1. In a small bowl, combine 2 tablespoons of the grainy mustard and the Dijon mustard. Put the bread crumbs into a shallow bowl and season with salt and pepper. Brush the mustard mixture over both sides of the chicken and evenly coat with the seasoned crumbs. Place the chicken in a single layer on a baking sheet, cover with plastic wrap, and refrigerate for at least 30 minutes or for up to several hours.

2. Preheat the oven to 200°F.

3. In a large skillet, heat 1 tablespoon of the oil and 1 tablespoon of the butter over medium-high heat. Cook the chicken in batches, for about 7 minutes on each side, or until golden brown and cooked through, adding additional oil if needed and transferring the chicken to a baking sheet. Put the chicken into the oven to keep warm.

4. Meanwhile, melt the remaining 1 tablespoon butter in the skillet. Add the mushrooms and all but 1 tablespoon of the scallions and cook, stirring, over medium heat for 4 to 6 minutes, until the mushrooms are golden brown. Add the wine and broth and cook until the liquid is reduced by half, scraping with a wooden spoon to loosen any browned bits in the bottom of the skillet. Stir in the cream and simmer until slightly thickened. Stir in the remaining 2 tablespoons grainy mustard, increase the heat to high, and boil gently for 4 minutes, or until the sauce is slightly thickened. Season with lemon juice, salt, and pepper.

5. Transfer the chicken to a platter. Spoon the sauce over it, sprinkle with the remaining 1 tablespoon scallions, and serve.

S E R V E S 6

oven-fried *Lemon* chicken

Lemon, yogurt, and ground red pepper flavor and tenderize this subtly spiced, no-fuss chicken dish. If you wish, bake the chicken in the morning and refrigerate, covered. Set the chicken out about 30 minutes before serving, or recrisp in a 350°F oven for about 15 minutes. This is ideal food for a large gathering. The ingredients are easily doubled or tripled for the same zesty results.

1 (8-ounce) container plain low-fat yogurt

1 large egg

1 teaspoon grated lemon zest

2 tablespoons fresh lemon juice

Salt and freshly ground pepper

1/8 teaspoon ground red pepper

1 (3 1/2-pound) chicken, cut into
    8 pieces, skin removed

1 1/2 cups dried bread crumbs

1/4 cup olive or vegetable oil

1. In a large bowl, whisk together the yogurt, egg, lemon zest and juice, 1/2 teaspoon salt, 1/2 teaspoon pepper, and the ground red pepper.

2. Add the chicken to the yogurt mixture, turning to coat well. Cover and refrigerate for at least 1 or up to 4 hours.

3. Preheat the oven to 425°F. Generously oil a jelly-roll or roasting pan.

4. Spread the bread crumbs in a pie plate. Roll the chicken pieces in the crumbs to coat, pressing so the crumbs adhere.

5. In a large heavy skillet, heat 2 tablespoons of the oil over high heat. Add half the chicken and cook for about 2 minutes on each side, or until browned. Transfer the chicken to the prepared pan and repeat with the remaining chicken and oil.

6. Bake the chicken for 35 to 40 minutes, until cooked through. Serve hot or at room temperature.

S E R V E S 4

Tailgate Picnic

Picnic Potato Salad
page 108

Oven-Fried Lemon Chicken

Confetti Cole Slaw
page 105

Scalloped Summer
Tomatoes
page 96

Buttermilk-Scallion
Drop Biscuits
page 99

Blackberry Lemonade

Chocolate Pan Cake
page 114

mediterranean Chicken

t his robust chicken dish takes advantage of the high-quality flavored olive oils—garlic, basil, rosemary, and lemon—found in most supermarkets. These oils pack a lot of flavor. Drizzle them on soups, salads, grilled breads, or vegetables to give favorite foods a lift. During the warmer weather, grill the chicken, adding a handful of your favorite wood chips to the fire.

main courses

4 skinless boneless chicken breast halves (about
   5 ounces each)
Salt and freshly ground pepper
2 tablespoons olive oil, preferably garlic-flavored
1 cup canned chicken broth
1/4 cup pitted oil-cured black olives, chopped
1/4 cup oil-packed sun-dried tomatoes, drained
   and chopped
2 tablespoons chopped fresh parsley

1. Season the chicken on both sides with salt and pepper. In a large heavy skillet, heat the oil over medium-high heat until very hot but not smoking. Add the chicken and cook, turning once, for 10 to 12 minutes, until just cooked through. Transfer to a plate and cover to keep warm.

2. Add the broth, olives, sun-dried tomatoes, 1 tablespoon of the parsley, and salt and pepper to taste to the skillet and bring to a boil. Add any accumulated juices from the chicken and cook the mixture for 3 to 5 minutes, until the sauce has begun to reduce and becomes slightly syrupy. Remove from the heat.

3. To serve, place the chicken on plates, spoon the sauce over it, and sprinkle with the remaining 1 tablespoon parsley.
S E R V E S   4

chicken tetrazzini with two Cheeses

Over the years, many delicious dishes have been created and named after famous people—especially European opera stars. Chicken Tetrazzini, named in honor of the Italian diva Luisa Tetrazzini, is a flavorful combination of pasta, chicken, mushrooms, and cheese sauce and, incidentally, is a great way to use up leftover pasta and chicken. It's perfect for an informal dinner with friends—round out the meal with some crusty bread and a tomato, black olive, and arugula salad drizzled with balsamic dressing.

8 ounces spaghetti, broken in half

4 teaspoons olive oil

1/2 pound white mushrooms, quartered

2 garlic cloves, minced

3/4 cup thinly sliced scallions

1/4 cup cornstarch

1/4 cup medium-dry sherry

2 cups milk

1 1/2 cups chicken broth

1/2 cup grated Jarlsburg or Swiss cheese

1/3 cup freshly grated Parmesan cheese

Salt and freshly ground pepper

2 1/2 cups shredded cooked chicken or turkey

1/3 cup fresh bread crumbs

1. Bring a large pot of water to a boil over high heat. Add a large pinch of salt and the spaghetti and cook, stirring often, for 9 to 10 minutes, until al dente. Drain the pasta in a colander and toss with a little of the oil; set aside.

2. Preheat the oven to 450°F. Spray a shallow 2-quart baking dish with nonstick cooking spray.

3. In a medium nonstick skillet, heat 2 teaspoons of the oil over high heat. Add the mushrooms and garlic and cook, stirring, for 4 minutes, or until the mushrooms are lightly browned. Stir in the scallions and cook, stirring, for 1 to 2 minutes longer, until the scallions are wilted. Remove from the heat.

4. In a small cup, blend the cornstarch with the sherry until smooth. In a large pot, stir together the milk, broth, and the cornstarch mixture. Place over medium heat and cook, stirring, until the sauce thickens and boils. Remove from the heat and add the Jarlsburg, about half of the Parmesan, 1 teaspoon salt, and 1/2 teaspoon pepper, stirring until well blended. Stir in the chicken and the mushrooms, then stir in the spaghetti. Transfer the mixture to the prepared baking dish.

5. In a small bowl, mix the bread crumbs with the remaining Parmesan and the remaining 2 teaspoons oil and sprinkle over the casserole. Bake for 10 to 15 minutes, until the top is browned and the casserole is bubbly.

SERVES 4 TO 6

warm chicken Waldorf salad

Waldorf salad was born around the turn of the century at the famed Waldorf-Astoria Hotel, where the combination of apples, celery, and mayonnaise, served on a bed of lettuce, was an instant hit. With the addition of Deli-roasted chicken, this classic becomes particularly elegant and tasty—perfect for a casual spring luncheon.

main courses

1 red or green apple, halved, cored, and
  finely chopped
1 celery stalk with leaves, finely chopped
1/4 cup chopped walnuts, preferably toasted
1/4 cup golden raisins
2 tablespoons chopped fresh parsley
1 cup mayonnaise
Salt and freshly ground pepper
1 (2-pound) Deli-roasted chicken,
  kept warm
About 6 cups mixed salad greens,
  for serving

1. In a large bowl, stir together the apple, celery, walnuts, raisins, parsley, and mayonnaise. Season with salt and pepper.
2. With your fingers, finely shred the chicken, discarding the skin and bones. Stir the chicken into the apple mixture.
3. Arrange the salad greens on a platter or four serving plates. Spoon the chicken salad onto the greens and serve.

SERVES 4

Springtime Lunch

Roasted Asparagus with Lemon
and Pine Nuts
page 84

Warm Chicken Waldorf
Salad

Red & Green Grapes

Dinner rolls

Zucchini-Lemon
Quick Bread
page 122

grilled chicken with Tomatoes & goat cheese

the success of this unusually simple grilled chicken dish depends on using the freshest and most flavorful ingredients. A lively balsamic dressing enriches and intensifies the tomatoes, which deliciously contrast with the creamy, mild-tasting goat cheese.

**4 whole chicken breasts
(about 2 1/4 pounds), split
1/4 cup plus 2 tablespoons
olive oil
Salt and freshly ground pepper
1 tablespoon plus 1 teaspoon balsamic
vinegar
4 small tomatoes, seeded and chopped
1/4 cup chopped fresh parsley
1 (3 1/2- to 4-ounce) package soft
goat cheese**

1. Preheat the grill to hot or preheat the broiler.

2. Brush the chicken on both sides with 2 tablespoons of the oil and season with salt and pepper.

3. Grill the breasts, skin side down, for 10 to 12 minutes, until the skin is crisp and browned. Turn the chicken and cook for 10 to 15 minutes longer, until nicely browned on both sides and cooked through.

4. Meanwhile, put the vinegar in a medium bowl and slowly whisk in the remaining 1/4 cup oil. Stir in the tomatoes and parsley and season with salt and pepper.

5. To serve, place the chicken on plates, spoon the tomato mixture over, and crumble the goat cheese on top.

SERVES 4

main courses

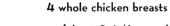

42

turkey Know how

When it comes to roasting turkey, there are no hard and fast rules. Whether you roast turkey covered or uncovered, at high or moderate temperature, or baste frequently or infrequently, is a matter of personal preference. ❧ Fresh turkeys are a good choice over the frozen variety, and there are several reasons why. You don't need to set aside thawing time, the turkey can be purchased right before you plan to roast it, and most importantly, fresh turkeys retain more of their natural juices, so the resulting bird is much moister. ❧ From one year to the next it is hard to remember what size turkey to purchase. So here's the basic rule of thumb: When a turkey weighs twelve pounds or less, allow three-quarters to one pound of meat per person. Turkeys that weigh more than twelve pounds are a little meatier, so you need slightly less weight per person. ❧ Lastly, it is important for a turkey to be thoroughly cooked, including the stuffing. Use the turkey timetable (see below), as a guide and roast the turkey until an instant-read thermometer inserted into the thickest part of the thigh (away from the bone) registers 180°. If the turkey is stuffed, the stuffing should read 165°.

Thanksgiving
❧
Roasted Red Pepper Soup
page 21

Holiday Turkey
with Apple-Pear Stuffing
page 45

Cauliflower
with Parmesan Crumbs
page 86

Fresh Cranberry
Sauce

Garlic Mashed Potato Casserole
page 91

Brown
Sugar Pumpkin Pie
page 128

Turkey Roasting Timetable

Weight	*Unstuffed*	*Stuffed*
8 to 12 pounds	3 to 4 hours	3 1/2 to 4 1/2 hours
12 to 16 pounds	3 1/2 to 4 1/2 hours	4 1/2 to 5 1/2 hours
16 to 20 pounds	4 to 5 hours	5 1/2 to 6 1/2 hours
20 to 24 pounds	4 1/2 to 5 1/2 hours	6 1/2 to 7 hours

holiday turkey with
Apple-pear stuffing

perfectly roasted turkey always makes a dramatic centerpiece for a holiday meal. The apple-pear stuffing, a rich, flavorful blend of traditional and new ingredients, such as sour cherries and dried pears, sets this recipe apart. Prepare it one day ahead, but stuff the turkey just before it goes into the oven.

1 (14-pound) turkey

Salt and freshly ground pepper

APPLE-PEAR STUFFING

1/2 cup (1 stick) unsalted butter

4 Granny Smith apples, peeled, cored, and chopped

2 cups chopped onions

3 celery stalks with leaves, chopped

6 dried pear halves, chopped

1/2 cup golden raisins

1/2 cup dried sour cherries

36 slices firm white bread (about 2 pounds),
    cut into 3/4-inch squares

1/2 cup chopped fresh parsley

2 teaspoons fresh thyme leaves or
    3/4 teaspoon dried

1/2 teaspoon shredded fresh sage leaves
    or 1/4 teaspoon dried, crumbled

Salt and freshly ground pepper

1/2 cup turkey or chicken broth

1. Rinse the turkey inside and out and pat dry with paper towels. Season all over with salt and pepper. Place the turkey, breast side up, on a rack in a large roasting pan. Refrigerate.

2. Preheat the oven to 350°F.

3. In a large skillet, melt the butter over medium heat. Add the apples, onions, and celery and cook, stirring occasionally, for 8 minutes, or until softened. Transfer to a large bowl.

4. Add the dried pears, raisins, dried cherries, bread, parsley, thyme, and sage to the apple mixture and season with salt and pepper. Pour the broth over and toss until evenly moistened.

5. Spoon the stuffing loosely into the neck and body cavities. Place the remaining stuffing in a small buttered baking dish; refrigerate. Tuck the turkey skin at the neck end under, fold the wings under, and tie the legs together. Cover with a foil tent.

6. Roast the turkey for 2 3/4 hours, basting every 30 minutes with the pan juices. Remove the foil and continue roasting for about 45 minutes longer, or until an instant-read thermometer inserted into the thickest part of the thigh, away from the bone, registers 180°F. Let the turkey stand loosely covered with foil for about 20 minutes before carving.

7. Meanwhile, about 45 minutes before the turkey is done, put the reserved stuffing into the oven and bake for 1 hour.

8. Carve the turkey, spoon the stuffing into a bowl, and serve.

SERVES 10

diner-style Meatloaf

m eatloaf is the quintessential American comfort food, and this version is special enough to be served at any family gathering. All the robust flavor of the classic meatloaf has been left in, but the calories have been lightened by using ground turkey instead of beef. Sauteed shallots, carrots, and mushrooms, plus a touch of sage, makes it extra savory. As with all meatloaf, this makes super leftovers and, of course, great sandwiches.

1/2 cup chicken broth

1 tablespoon vegetable oil

3 large shallots, finely chopped

1/2 cup finely chopped carrot

10 ounces small white mushrooms,
   finely chopped

2 garlic cloves, minced

1 teaspoon salt

1/2 teaspoon freshly ground pepper

1 pound lean ground turkey

1 1/4 cups fresh bread crumbs

1 Granny Smith apple, peeled
   and grated

1/4 cup finely chopped fresh parsley

1 tablespoon finely chopped fresh sage
   leaves or 1 teaspoon dried,
   crumbled

1 large egg, lightly beaten

1. In a large nonstick skillet, bring the broth and oil to a simmer over medium-high heat. Add the shallots and carrot and cook, stirring, for about 4 minutes, or until the shallots are softened. Add the mushrooms, garlic, 1 teaspoon salt, and 1/2 teaspoon pepper and cook, stirring, for 5 minutes, or until most of the liquid has evaporated. Transfer the mixture to a large bowl and let cool.

2. Preheat the oven to 350°F. Lightly oil a baking sheet.

3. With your hands, thoroughly mix the turkey, bread crumbs, apple, parsley, and sage into the cooled vegetable mixture. Add the egg and mix well. Divide the mixture in half and on the baking sheet, shape each portion into an oval about 6 1/2 inches long, 4 inches wide, and 1 1/2 inches high. Transfer the loaves to the baking sheet.

4. Bake for about 45 minutes, or until cooked through. Let the meatloaf rest, loosely covered, for 5 minutes.

5. Cut the meatloaf into 1/2-inch slices, arrange on a platter, and serve. **SERVES 6**

main courses

filet mignon with Wild mushrooms

f or a special occasion, an anniversary, or other celebration, when nothing but the very best will do, filet mignon is an excellent choice. This special cut of beef is simple to prepare and prized for its buttery tenderness and low fat content. Here, a topping of wild mushrooms contributes a deep, earthy flavor while the creamy sauce only adds to the feeling of extravagance. Try a mix of shiitake, cremini, and oyster mushrooms, or experiment with any other variety your market carries.

5 tablespoons olive oil

1 1/4 pounds mixed white and wild mushrooms, thickly sliced

Salt and freshly ground pepper

6 center cut beef filet steaks (7 to 8 ounces each)

1 teaspoon Kosher salt

1 1/2 teaspoons coarsely ground pepper

2 tablespoons unsalted butter

2 large shallots, minced (about 1/4 cup)

1 garlic clove, minced

2 tablespoons Cognac or brandy

1 cup heavy cream

main courses

1. In a large heavy skillet, heat 2 tablespoons of the oil over high heat. Add the mushrooms and season with salt and pepper. Cook, stirring, for 6 to 8 minutes, until the mushrooms are well browned and the juices begin to evaporate. Pour the mushroom juices into a small dish and set aside. Remove the skillet from the heat and cover the mushrooms to keep warm.

2. Season the steaks with the Kosher salt and coarse pepper, pressing the seasonings into the surface of the meat.

3. In one or two large heavy skillets, heat the remaining 3 tablespoons oil over high heat until very hot but not smoking. Add the steaks and cook for 3 to 4 minutes on each side for medium-rare, or to the desired degree of doneness, reducing the heat if necessary. Transfer the steaks to a platter and cover loosely to keep warm.

4. Pour off the fat from the skillet, then melt the butter over medium heat. Add the shallots and garlic and cook until the shallots are softened, scraping with a wooden spoon to loosen any browned bits in the bottom of the pan. Add the brandy and the reserved mushroom juices and cook over medium-high heat for 1 minute, or until slightly thickened. Stir in the cream and any accumulated juices from the steaks and cook, stirring often, for 3 to 4 minutes, until the cream has thickened slightly. Season with salt and pepper if needed. Add the mushrooms and cook briefly to heat through.

5. Place the steaks on serving plates, spoon the mushroom sauce on top, and serve. **SERVES 6**

fireside Short ribs

beef short ribs, great for casual get-togethers, are back in vogue. These cuts of meat benefit from long, slow cooking in lots of liquid—they turn out meltingly tender, juicy, and full of flavor. Although they take several hours to cook, short ribs require no attention at all—so put your feet up and relax while they simmer away.

3 pounds boneless beef chuck short ribs,
　　cut into 3-inch pieces
Salt and freshly ground pepper
3 tablespoons olive oil
3 large leeks (white part only), halved lengthwise,
　　thinly sliced, washed thoroughly, and dried
3 carrots, halved lengthwise and cut diagonally
　　into 1-inch pieces
2 celery stalks with leaves, cut diagonally into
　　3/4-inch pieces
4 garlic cloves, 3 thinly sliced and 1 left whole
2 strips lemon zest (removed with a
　　vegetable peeler)
1 bay leaf
1/2 teaspoon dried thyme, crumbled
1 (16-ounce) can whole tomatoes in thick puree
1 (14 1/2-ounce) can beef broth plus
　　enough water to equal 2 cups, plus
　　additional if needed
1 cup dry red wine

3 tablespoons chopped fresh parsley
2 tablespoons fresh lemon juice
1 pound wide egg noodles, cooked
　　according to package directions
　　and kept warm

1. Preheat the broiler. Arrange the ribs in a single layer on a broiler pan and season with salt and pepper. Broil the ribs 4 to 6 inches from the heat for about 4 minutes on each side, or until well browned.

2. Preheat the oven to 350°F.

3. In a Dutch oven, heat the oil over medium-high heat. Add the leeks, carrots, celery, the sliced garlic, 1 strip of the lemon zest, the bay leaf, and thyme. Cook, stirring occasionally, for 4 minutes, or until the leeks are softened. Add the tomatoes, broth mixture, and wine and bring to a boil. Add the ribs and season with salt and pepper.

4. Cover the pot and place in the oven. Cook, turning the ribs every hour, for 2 1/2 hours, or until the meat is very tender, adding additional broth or water if the mixture seems dry. Skim off the fat and discard the bay leaf and lemon zest.

5. Meanwhile, mince together the remaining strip of lemon zest and the remaining garlic clove.

6. Add the minced zest and garlic to the pot along with 2 tablespoons of the parsley and the lemon juice. Season to taste with salt and pepper.

7. To serve, arrange the noodles on a platter, top with the short ribs and sauce, and sprinkle with the remaining 1 tablespoon parsley. **SERVES 8**

mom's best beef Stew

t his home-style stew brings back memories of childhood. Prepare it a day ahead so all the luscious flavors have a chance to develop, and be sure to serve it with the Buttermilk-Scallion Drop Biscuits—they're perfect for sopping up the delicious juices. Like most one-pot dishes, this recipe is easily doubled, so it's perfect for a crowd. The stew freezes well: Simply divide into easy-to-serve portions and it will keep for up to three months.

1/2 cup all-purpose flour

1 teaspoon paprika

Salt and freshly ground pepper

2 pounds well-trimmed beef chuck,
    cut into 1 1/4-inch chunks

About 1/4 cup olive oil

1 large onion, chopped, plus
    4 small onions,
    each cut into 6 wedges

4 garlic cloves, minced

3/4 teaspoon dried thyme, crumbled

3 bay leaves

1 (14 1/2-ounce) can beef broth

1 (14 1/2-ounce) can
    stewed tomatoes

1 1/2 cups water

1 pound new potatoes, cut into
    1-inch chunks

1/2 medium butternut squash, peeled,
    seeded, and cut into 1-inch chunks
    (about 2 cups)

2 large carrots, cut into 1/2-inch slices

Buttermilk-Scallion Drop Biscuits (p. 99)

1. In a large bowl, mix the flour, paprika, 1/2 teaspoon salt, and 3/4 teaspoon pepper. Add the beef and toss until coated.

2. In a Dutch oven, heat 2 tablespoons of the oil over medium-high heat. Cook the beef, in small batches, for 3 to 4 minutes, until lightly browned on all sides, adding additional oil as needed. Set aside the remaining seasoned flour.

3. Reduce the heat to medium and add the chopped onion, garlic, thyme, and bay leaves. Pour in 1/4 cup of the broth and cook, scraping with a wooden spoon to loosen any browned bits in the bottom of the pan. Cook, stirring, for 3 to 4 minutes, until the onion is tender, adding additional broth if the pot becomes dry. Stir in the reserved seasoned flour and cook, stirring constantly, for 1 minute.

4. Add the tomatoes and stir until the mixture begins to boil. Add the remaining broth, the water, and beef, along with any accumulated meat juices and bring to a boil. Reduce the heat to low. Cover and simmer for about 1 1/2 hours, or until the meat is just tender when pierced with a fork.

5. Add the potatoes, onion wedges, squash, and carrots and return the stew to a simmer. Cover and cook for 30 to 40 minutes longer, until the beef and vegetables are very tender. Serve the stew accompanied by the Scallion Drop Biscuits.

S E R V E S   4   T O   6

sunday Pot roast

pot roast is good food for relaxed, cozy weekend suppers in the kitchen. It's warming and indisputably appetizing when freshly baked, makes great leftovers, and is a super sandwich treat when thinly sliced and spread with mayonnaise or mustard. Mashed potatoes is the side dish of choice here. And don't forget to spoon some of the rich gravy on top.

main courses

1 teaspoon dried thyme, crumbled

Salt and freshly ground pepper

1 (2 1/2- to 3-pound)

    boneless beef chuck shoulder roast,

    trimmed

2 tablespoons olive oil

4 medium onions, halved and thinly sliced

6 garlic cloves, thinly sliced

3/4 cup canned crushed tomatoes

1 (14 1/2-ounce) can beef broth

1 1/4 cups water

3/4 cup dry red wine

2 bay leaves

3 tablespoons all-purpose flour

1. Preheat the oven to 325°F.

2. In a small bowl, mix the thyme, 1/2 teaspoon salt, and 1/2 teaspoon pepper. Rub all over the meat. Tie the roast with kitchen string. Set aside.

3. In a Dutch oven, heat the oil over medium heat. Add the onions, garlic, and 1/4 teaspoon salt and cook, stirring, for 6 to 8 minutes, until the onions are softened. Add the tomatoes, broth, 1 cup of the water, the wine, and bay leaves. Increase the heat to high and bring to a boil. Add the meat, cover the pot tightly, and transfer to the oven.

4. Bake for 2 1/2 to 3 hours, until the meat is tender. Transfer the meat to a platter and cover loosely with foil.

5. Discard the bay leaves and skim off the fat. Bring the liquid to a boil over medium heat. In a small cup, blend the flour and the remaining 1/4 cup water until smooth and slowly whisk into the bubbling liquid. Reduce the heat to low and simmer, stirring often, for 5 minutes, or until thickened. Pour any accumulated juices from the roast into the pot. Return the gravy to a simmer and season with salt and pepper if needed.

6. Remove the string from the roast, thinly slice the meat against the grain, arrange on a platter, and spoon some of the gravy on top. Transfer the remaining gravy to a sauceboat and pass it separately.

SERVES 4 TO 6

provençale Beef stew

elegant and rich-tasting, this stew is very different from the hearty, beefy-flavored versions Americans know so well. This fragrant stew is inspired by the flavors of Provence, a region of southeastern France. There, tomatoes, garlic, onion, orange zest, herbs, and even lavender give much of the food its unique appeal.

About 4 tablespoons butter

3 pounds boneless beef chuck,
   cut into 1-inch cubes

2 small onions, quartered and sliced

6 fresh flat-leaf parsley sprigs

2 strips orange zest (removed with a
   vegetable peeler)

1/4 teaspoon dried thyme, crumbled

1/4 teaspoon dried rosemary, crumbled

2 bay leaves

1 1/2 cups dry red wine

1 1/2 cups chicken broth

1 cup water

4 garlic cloves, minced

Salt and freshly ground pepper

1/2 pound baby carrots

2 small turnips, peeled and cut into
   1/2-inch chunks

1/2 pound pearl onions, peeled

18 medium asparagus spears, trimmed and
   cut diagonally into 2-inch lengths

2 teaspoons sugar

1. In a Dutch oven, melt 2 tablespoons of the butter over medium heat. Cook the beef, in batches, for about 4 minutes, or until browned on all sides, adding additional oil as needed. Set the beef aside in a large bowl. Add the onions to the pot and cook, stirring frequently, for 5 minutes, or until softened.

2. Return the beef to the pot. Add the parsley sprigs, orange zest, thyme, rosemary, bay leaves, wine, broth, and water and bring to a boil over high heat. Reduce the heat to low, cover, and simmer for 15 minutes. Add the garlic, 1/2 teaspoon salt, and 1/4 teaspoon pepper and simmer, covered, for 30 minutes longer.

3. Add the carrots, turnips, and pearl onions to the pot and cook, partially covered, for about 30 minutes. Stir in the asparagus and cook for 10 minutes longer, or until the beef and vegetables are tender.

4. With a slotted spoon, transfer the meat and vegetables to a large serving bowl and cover to keep warm. Boil the stew liquid over medium-high heat for about 10 minutes, or until thickened. Discard the parsley sprigs, orange zest, and bay leaves. Stir in the sugar and season with salt if needed. Spoon the sauce over the beef and vegetables and serve.

S E R V E S   6   T O   8

chunky beef Chili

C hili is great party food. It's easy to prepare for a crowd and is the kind of food that lends itself to a "help yourself" style of serving, especially at an informal gathering like a Super Bowl Sunday party. Set out lots of colorful toppings, such as several kinds of shredded cheese, diced avocado and bell pepper, chopped red onion, crisp-fried tortilla strips, chopped cilantro, sour cream, and a variety of hot sauces. Then let your guests create their own personalized "bowls of red."

About 1/4 cup vegetable oil

1 1/2 pounds well-trimmed beef chuck,
  cut into 3/4-inch chunks

3 large onions, coarsely chopped

5 garlic cloves, minced

1/4 cup chili powder

1 tablespoon plus 1 teaspoon ground cumin

1 1/2 teaspoons ground coriander

1/2 teaspoon dried oregano, crumbled

Salt and freshly ground pepper

1 (14 1/2-ounce) can Mexican-style
  stewed tomatoes

1 (14 1/2-ounce) can beef broth

1 1/2 cups water

1 teaspoon Tabasco sauce

Monterey Jack and Jalapeño Corn Bread (p. 98)

Hot cooked rice, for serving

1. In a Dutch oven, heat the oil over medium-high heat. Cook the beef, in batches, for about 3 minutes, or until lightly browned on all sides, adding additional oil if needed. Transfer the beef to a medium bowl.

2. Add the onions and garlic to the pot and cook, stirring, for 3 to 4 minutes, until the onions are softened. Stir in the chili powder, cumin, coriander, oregano, 1/2 teaspoon salt, and 1/2 teaspoon pepper and cook, stirring constantly, for about 30 seconds, or until the spices are very fragrant.

3. Return the beef to the pot. Add the stewed tomatoes, broth, water, and Tabasco and bring to a boil. Reduce the heat to low and simmer, partially covered, for about 1 1/2 hours, or until the meat is very tender.

4. Serve the chili accompanied by the Monterey Jack and Jalapeño Corn Bread and rice.

S E R V E S   4   T O   6

main courses

main courses

lamb with roasted Vegetables

S erve this tempting dish at Easter, when lamb is at its tender best. Here, the meat is roasted until medium (pink throughout). But if you prefer your lamb well done, it will be just as delicious—the meat will caramelize and become deliciously crusty from the extra time in the oven. Serve with steamed asparagus and scalloped potatoes.

I pound shiitake mushrooms, stems
 removed and caps sliced

2 yellow bell peppers, cored, seeded,
 and thinly sliced

4 garlic cloves, quartered

I (28-ounce) can whole tomatoes,
 drained and coarsely chopped

1/4 cup olive oil

Salt and freshly ground pepper

I bone-in leg of lamb
 (about 7 1/2 pounds),
 excess fat trimmed

1/2 teaspoon dried rosemary,
 crumbled

1/2 teaspoon dried thyme, crumbled

2 tablespoons chopped fresh parsley

1. Preheat the oven to 450°F.

2. In the center of a large roasting pan, toss together the mushrooms, bell peppers, garlic, tomatoes, and 2 tablespoons of the oil. Season with salt and pepper and place the lamb on top of the vegetables. Drizzle the remaining 2 tablespoons oil over the lamb, sprinkle with the rosemary and thyme, and season with salt and pepper.

3. Roast the lamb for 15 minutes. Reduce the temperature to 375°F and continue roasting, basting every 30 minutes with the pan juices, for 1 1/2 hours longer, until an instant-read thermometer registers 140°F for medium, or to the desired degree of doneness.

4. Transfer the lamb to a cutting board, cover loosely with foil, and let rest for 10 to 20 minutes. Stir 1 tablespoon of the parsley into the vegetables in the roasting pan, then cover to keep warm.

S E R V E S   8

herb-grilled Leg of lamb

main courses

Outdoor entertaining doesn't get simpler than placing a well-marinated piece of lamb on the grill. If you can't find butterflied lamb in the meat section of your supermarket, pick out the nicest looking bone-in leg of lamb you can find, and ask the butcher to butterfly it for you. If you plan on inviting upwards of ten guests, buy a whole leg and double the marinade. And for the richest flavor, marinate the meat overnight.

3 tablespoons olive oil

3 tablespoons fresh lemon juice

4 large garlic cloves, slivered

1 1/2 teaspoons dried rosemary, crumbled

1 teaspoon dried thyme, crumbled

1 teaspoon dried oregano, crumbled

Freshly ground pepper

1 shank portion leg of lamb, boned, butterflied, and
    excess fat trimmed (2 to 2 1/2 pounds)

Salt

1. In a small bowl, mix the oil, lemon juice, garlic, rosemary, thyme, oregano, and 1/2 teaspoon pepper. Put the lamb into a baking dish and spread the herb mixture over the lamb. Cover and marinate in the refrigerator for at least 3 hours, or overnight.

2. Preheat the grill to medium-hot.

3. Season the lamb on both sides with 1/2 teaspoon salt. Grill, turning once or twice, for 30 to 40 minutes, until a meat ther-mometer inserted into the thickest part of the lamb registers 130°F for medium rare, or to the desired degree of doneness.

4. Remove the lamb from the grill and let rest, loosely covered with foil, for about 10 minutes.

5. Using a sharp thin knife, cut the lamb into thin slices, and arrange on a platter, and serve. **SERVES 4 TO 6**

Backyard Buffet

Mixed Olives

Flaky Cheddar Biscuits
page 10

Baby Greens Salad with Fresh
Chopped Herbs

Roasted Garlic and Red Wine
Vinaigrette
page 101

Herb-Grilled Leg of Lamb

Parmesan-Glazed
Tomatoes
page 97

Best-Ever
Devil's Food Cake
page 115

lamb with sage & White beans

this is a terrific take-along dish for autumn potluck parties and church suppers. It reheats well and tastes even better the next day. Shoulder and round-bone lamb chops, which are not as tender but are more flavorful than rib or loin chops, benefit from the long, slow cooking. Serve in over-sized soup plates with lots of crusty bread to soak up the delicious rich juices.

4 garlic cloves

Kosher salt

3/4 teaspoon dried rosemary

3/4 teaspoon dried sage

1/2 teaspoon dried thyme

1/2 teaspoon ground ginger

Freshly ground pepper

2 tablespoons olive oil,
   preferably extra-virgin

6 shoulder or round-bone lamb chops
   (about 2 1/2 pounds), excess
   fat trimmed

1 (16-ounce) can crushed tomatoes

1 cup chicken broth

1/3 cup dry red wine

1 bay leaf

1 (19-ounce) can cannellini beans,
   rinsed and drained

Salt

1. Preheat the broiler. Lightly oil the broiler pan.

2. Coarsely chop the garlic. Sprinkle with 3/4 teaspoon Kosher salt and mash the garlic with the flat side of a large knife to form a paste. Chop in the rosemary, sage, thyme, ginger, and 1/2 teaspoon pepper until well blended. Scrape the mixture into a small dish and stir in the oil.

3. Rub the herb mixture onto both sides of the chops. Broil the chops 4 inches from the heat source, turning once, for 5 to 7 minutes per side, until lightly browned. Remove from the heat.

4. In a large deep skillet or Dutch oven, combine the tomatoes, broth, wine, and bay leaf and bring to a boil over high heat. Add the chops and any accumulated juices to the skillet. Return to a boil. Reduce the heat to low, cover, and simmer for 1 hour, or until the lamb is very tender when pierced with a fork.

5. Add the beans, cover, and simmer for 15 minutes longer. Remove the bay leaf, season with salt and pepper if needed, and serve. **SERVES 4 TO 6**

fruit-stuffed Loin of pork

pork and prunes are a match made in heaven. This is a spectacular boneless roast to serve at a large dinner party, where it will undoubtedly impress your guests. Stuff and roll the pork in the morning, then cover and refrigerate until one and a half hours before serving. The meat is easy to slice, and the fruit-filled center is impressive-looking. Serve accompanied by wild rice and either steamed spinach or Swiss chard.

2 tablespoons butter

3 small shallots, finely chopped

3 garlic cloves, minced

2 teaspoons fresh thyme leaves

1/2 cup apple cider or apple juice

1 cup pitted prunes

12 dried apricot halves, thinly sliced

2 thin slices lemon

Salt and freshly ground pepper

1 1/2 teaspoons fennel seeds, crushed

1 (4-pound) center cut boneless pork loin, butterflied and excess fat trimmed

1. Preheat the oven to 325°F. Place a rack in the middle of the oven.

2. In a medium saucepan, melt the butter over low heat. Add the shallots, garlic, and thyme and cook, stirring, for 3 minutes, or until the shallots are softened. Add the apple cider and bring to a boil. Add the prunes, apricots, lemon slices, 1/4 teaspoon salt, and 1/4 teaspoon pepper and stir to combine. Remove the pan from the heat, cover, and let stand for about 10 minutes.

3. With a mortar and pestle or in a spice grinder, grind the fennel seeds to a powder.

4. Place the pork loin on a work surface fat side down with a long side facing you and the thicker, meatier edge away from you. Sprinkle the pork with 1/4 teaspoon salt, 1/4 teaspoon pepper, and the ground fennel. Spoon the fruit mixture onto the pork, forming a 2-inch-wide mound. Leave a 2-inch border along the edge closest to you and a 1 1/2-inch border along the other edges. Beginning with the edge closest to you, tightly roll up the pork jelly-roll style to form a cylinder. With kitchen string, tie the pork crosswise at 1-inch intervals.

5. Place the pork, seam side down, on a wire rack set in a roasting pan. Roast for 1 1/2 hours, or until an instant-read thermometer inserted into the center registers 145°F. Transfer the pork to a cutting board, cover with foil, and let stand for 10 minutes.

6. To serve, remove the string from the pork and, with a thin sharp knife, cut into 1/2-inch slices. **SERVES 10**

main courses

skillet supper Pork chops

b acon, apple, and cabbage are a great flavor combination that is traditional in Eastern Europe and maybe in your house, too. This dish tastes like it has simmered all day, but in fact it cooks fairly quickly and makes a great weeknight dish. Offer the chops with some robust mustard, thickly sliced whole-grain bread, and beer for a complete meal.

4 slices bacon, cut into

    1/2-inch strips

1/4 cup all-purpose flour

Salt and freshly ground pepper

Four 3/4-inch-thick boneless loin pork

    chops (about 4 ounces each)

2 tablespoons butter

1/2 cup chicken broth

6 cups finely shredded Savoy cabbage

    (about 1 pound)

1 McIntosh apple, cut into 1/2-inch

    wedges

1 tablespoon light brown sugar

1 teaspoon balsamic vinegar

1 teaspoon fresh thyme leaves or

    1/2 teaspoon dried

1 bay leaf

1 tablespoon snipped fresh chives or

    2 teaspoons freeze-dried

1. In a large deep skillet, cook the bacon over medium heat until crisp and browned. With a slotted spoon, transfer the bacon to a paper towel–lined plate. Set the skillet aside.

2. On a plate, combine the flour with 1/4 teaspoon salt and 1/4 teaspoon pepper. Lightly coat the pork with the seasoned flour, shaking off the excess.

3. Melt the butter in the same skillet over medium-high heat. Add the pork and cook, turning once, for 8 to 10 minutes, until well browned and just cooked through. Transfer the pork to a plate and cover to keep warm.

4. Pour the broth into the skillet. Add the cabbage, apple, brown sugar, vinegar, thyme, bay leaf, 1/4 teaspoon salt, and 1/4 teaspoon pepper. Cook, stirring frequently, for 6 minutes, or until the cabbage is wilted.

5. To serve, arrange the cabbage mixture on plates, top with the pork, and sprinkle with the bacon and chives.

S E R V E S   4

country Barbecued ribs

 ecause they're so tender and flavorful, baby back ribs are the preferred cut here. If you like, you can use regular spare ribs—they will take just a bit longer on the grill. Easily doubled or tripled, this recipe is great for a backyard party. Pile the ribs on several platters and set out generous bowls of Picnic Potato Salad (page 108) and Confetti Slaw (page 103). Serve with pitchers of homemade lemonade, iced tea, and cold beer.

SEASONING RUB

2 tablespoons chili powder

1 tablespoon ground cumin

1 teaspoon sugar

Kosher salt

Coarsely ground pepper

3 racks baby back ribs (about 1 pound
   each)

BASTING AND TABLE SAUCE

1 cup ketchup

1/4 cup packed brown sugar

1/4 cup cider vinegar

2 tablespoons fresh lemon juice

2 tablespoons molasses

1 teaspoon chili powder

1/4 teaspoon crushed red pepper flakes

1. In a small dish, mix together the chili powder, cumin, sugar, 2 teaspoons Kosher salt, and 1 teaspoon coarse pepper. Rub the mixture over both sides of the ribs. Wrap each rack of ribs in a generous sheet of heavy-duty foil and refrigerate for at least 8 hours, or overnight.

2. Preheat the grill to medium.

3. In a small saucepan, combine the ketchup, brown sugar, vinegar, lemon juice, molasses, chili powder, and red pepper flakes. Bring to a boil over medium heat; remove from the heat. Pour one third of the sauce into a small bowl and set the remainder aside.

4. Place the foil packets of ribs on the grill, leaving some space between them. Cover and grill, without turning, for 45 minutes, or until the ribs are tender when pierced with a fork.

5. Remove the ribs from the foil and place them on the grill. Grill, turning several times (moving the ribs to the outer edge of the grill to prevent burning if necessary) for 10 to 20 minutes longer, until the ribs are well browned.

6. Brush both sides of the ribs with the basting sauce, placing them curved side down. Cover and grill for 4 to 5 minutes. Turn the ribs curved side up and brush with sauce. Cover and grill for 2 to 3 minutes longer, until the ribs are well glazed.

7. Cut the racks in half and serve accompanied by the reserved table sauce. **SERVES 4 TO 6**

Marinades & Sauces

Everyone loves to grill, and marinating food beforehand gives it a wonderful depth of flavor and also tenderizes tougher cuts of meat. The longer meat or poultry marinates, the more the marinade flavor will come through. For the best results, marinate meat and poultry for at least two hours or overnight, but keep in mind that smaller pieces of meat absorb flavor more quickly than larger cuts.

classic chinese marinade

In a medium bowl, whisk together 1/2 cup hoisin sauce; 2 tablespoons ketchup;
2 tablespoons rice wine vinegar; 1 tablespoon soy sauce; 4 garlic cloves, slightly smashed;
and 1/4 teaspoon Tabasco sauce until blended. Refrigerate until ready to use.

MAKES ABOUT 1 CUP

teriyaki marinade

In a medium bowl, combine 3/4 cup soy sauce; 1/4 cup freshly grated peeled ginger;
4 garlic cloves, lightly smashed; 1 tablespoon rice wine vinegar; 1 teaspoon Dijon mustard; 1 teaspoon sugar;
and 1 teaspoon freshly ground pepper. Slowly pour in 1/4 cup light sesame or vegetable oil,
whisking constantly. Refrigerate until ready to use.

MAKES ABOUT 1 1/4 CUPS

lemon, mustard, and rosemary marinade

In a medium bowl, whisk 1/2 cup olive oil; 1/3 cup fresh lemon juice;

2 tablespoons grainy mustard; 1 tablespoon chopped fresh rosemary or 1 teaspoon dried rosemary;

and 1/2 teaspoon freshly ground pepper until well blended. Refrigerate until ready to use.

MAKES ABOUT 1 CUP

lime-cilantro marinade

In a medium bowl, combine 1/3 cup olive oil; 1/3 cup fresh lime juice; 2 garlic cloves, crushed with a

garlic press; 3 tablespoons finely chopped cilantro; 1 jalapeño pepper, seeded and minced;

2 to 3 teaspoons chili powder; and 2 teaspoons ground cumin, whisking until blended.

Season with salt and freshly ground pepper. Refrigerate until ready to use.

MAKES ABOUT 1 1/4 CUPS

double mustard marinade

In a medium bowl, whisk together 1/4 cup honey mustard; 1 tablespoon grainy mustard; 2 tablespoons white wine

vinegar; and 1/4 cup finely minced onion. Slowly pour in 1 cup extra-virgin olive oil, whisking constantly. Season

with salt and freshly ground pepper. Refrigerate until ready to use.

MAKES ABOUT 1 1/4 CUPS

the best BBQ sauce

In a medium bowl, whisk together 1 cup ketchup; 1 cup chile sauce; 1/4 cup honey;

3 tablespoons drained prepared horseradish; 2 tablespoons fresh lime juice; 2 tablespoons

Worcestershire sauce; 2 tablespoons molasses; 1 tablespoon Tabasco;

2 tablespoons dry mustard; and 4 garlic cloves, minced. Refrigerate until ready to use.

MAKES ABOUT 2 1/2 CUPS

citrus & pepper–rubbed Pork roast

t his impressive-looking citrus and rosemary–rubbed pork roast, surrounded by perfectly roasted apples, makes a spectacular centerpiece for Christmas Eve dinner or any other festive occasion. Frenching the bones (removing the meat surrounding the rib bones) makes the roast look especially elegant. (Ask your butcher to do it for you.) At the table, cut the uncarved roast into individual chops and serve. For an extra-special touch, add a splash of apple-flavored brandy to the pan while the pork is roasting, or cover the ends of the rib bones with paper frills (available in specialty food stores), before bringing the roast to the table.

CITRUS-PEPPER RUB

Zest of 2 medium lemons and 1 medium

    orange (removed in strips with a

    vegetable peeler)

10 garlic cloves

2 teaspoons dried rosemary

1 teaspoon dried sage

Coarsely ground pepper

2 tablespoons extra-virgin olive oil

One 8-rib pork rib roast (about 5 1/2 pounds),

    chine bone removed and bones frenched

    (see note above)

Kosher salt

Extra-virgin olive oil

APPLE-ONION MIXTURE

2 pounds lady apples, left whole, or sweet-tart

    red apples, such as Empire or Winesap,

    quartered and cored

2 medium onions, halved and sliced

1/3 cup chicken broth

2 tablespoons orange juice

1 tablespoon sugar

Salt and freshly ground pepper

PAN SAUCE

1 cup chicken broth

2 teaspoons cornstarch blended with 3 tablespoons

    heavy cream

1 tablespoon butter, cut into pieces

Salt and freshly ground pepper

1. Make the citrus-pepper rub. In a food processor, combine the lemon and orange zests, the garlic, rosemary, sage, 1 1/2 teaspoons coarse pepper, and the oil and process until the zests are finely chopped. Spread the mixture all over the pork, cover, and marinate in the refrigerator for at least 3 or for up to 8 hours.

2. Put the pork into an oiled roasting pan. Set aside.

3. Preheat the oven to 425°F.

4. Sprinkle 1 1/2 teaspoons Kosher salt over the pork and drizzle with 1 tablespoon oil. Roast for 15 minutes. Reduce the

oven temperature to 350°F and roast the pork for 30 minutes longer.

5. Meanwhile, prepare the apple-onion mixture. In a large bowl, toss together the apples, onions, broth, orange juice, sugar, and a pinch each of salt and pepper.

6. Move the pork to one side of the pan and spoon the apple mixture into the pan, mixing it with the pan juices. Roast the pork for 50 to 60 minutes longer, until an instant-read thermometer inserted into the center registers 155°F. Transfer the pork to a platter and cover. Transfer the apple mixture to a bowl and cover to keep warm.

7. Make the pan sauce. Spoon off the fat from the roasting pan. Add the broth to the pan and bring to a boil over medium heat, scraping with a wooden spoon to loosen any browned bits in the bottom of the pan. Pour the pan liquid into a medium saucepan. Add the cornstarch mixture and cook, whisking constantly, until the sauce thickens slightly and bubbles. Reduce the heat to low, whisk in the butter and cook, stirring constantly, until the sauce is thick and glossy. Pour in any accumulated juices from the pork and return the sauce to a simmer. Remove from the heat and season with salt and pepper if needed.

8. Using a sharp knife, cut the pork into individual chops. Arrange on a platter and spoon the apple mixture around the pork. Pass the sauce separately.

S E R V E S   8

main courses

Christmas Eve Dinner

Gravlax
with Mustard Sauce
page 15

Savory Stuffed
Mushrooms
page 12

Citrus and
Pepper-Rubbed Pork Roast
page 67

Garlic
Mashed Potato Casserole
page 91

Orange and
Honey-Glazed Carrots
page 86

Festive Breads

Cranberry-Tangerine
Cheesecake
page 121

Assorted Dessert Cookies

venison & black Bean chili

When a friendly neighbor offers to share some of his venison bounty with you, it's time to prepare this full-flavored and unusual chili. Any cut of venison will do—in fact, the tougher cuts of venison make extra tasty chili. This is Super Bowl Sunday food at its best. For the easiest grinding, make sure the meat is trimmed and well chilled. And for the most flavor, make the chili at least one day ahead—the flavors will have a chance to meld, and you won't have to miss a single touchdown.

About 1/4 cup olive oil

2 pounds venison stew meat,
    coarsely ground

2 large onions, coarsely chopped

4 slices bacon, cut into
    1/4-inch dice

8 garlic cloves, minced

2 large red bell peppers, cored,
    seeded and chopped

2 jalapeño peppers, 1 seeded,
    both finely chopped

1/4 cup chili powder

2 tablespoons ground cumin

Salt and freshly ground pepper

1/4 to 1/2 teaspoon ground red pepper

1 (15-ounce) can crushed tomatoes

1 (6-ounce) can tomato paste

1 (14 1/2-ounce) can chicken broth

1 1/2 cups dry red wine

1 cup water

2 (19-ounce) cans black beans, drained
    and rinsed

Sour cream, sliced scallions, and grated
    cheddar cheese, for serving

1. In a large Dutch oven, heat 2 tablespoons of the oil over high heat high until very hot but not smoking. Cook the venison in batches, for 3 minutes, or until browned, adding additional oil if needed. Transfer the meat to a bowl and pour off the fat.

2. Add 1 tablespoon of the oil, the onions, bacon, and garlic to the pot. Reduce the heat to medium and cook, stirring, for 6 to 8 minutes, until the onions are tender. Stir in the bell peppers and jalapeños and cook, stirring, for 4 minutes, or until softened. Stir in the chili powder, cumin, 1 1/2 teaspoons salt, 1 to 1 1/2 teaspoon pepper, and the ground red pepper and cook, stirring, for 1 minute, or until the spices are fragrant.

3. Stir in the tomatoes, tomato paste, venison and any accumulated juices, the broth, wine, and water. Bring to a boil, then reduce the heat to low. Cover and simmer, stirring occasionally, for 1 hour and 15 minutes. Add the beans and simmer for 15 minutes longer.

4. Serve the chili accompanied by sour cream, scallions, and cheese. **SERVES 8 TO 10**

main courses

shrimp with Creole sauce

the secret to memorable shrimp creole is to make sure the shrimp aren't overcooked or covered with too much sauce. Here, they are highly seasoned, then broiled and tossed with a light, savory tomato and bell pepper sauce, making this the best creole ever.

2 garlic cloves

Salt

1 tablespoon extra-virgin olive oil

1 teaspoon paprika

1/8 teaspoon dried thyme leaves,
   crumbled

1/8 teaspoon crushed red pepper flakes

1 1/2 pounds large shrimp, peeled and
   deveined

CREOLE SAUCE

1 tablespoon extra-virgin olive oil

1 each medium red and green bell pepper,
   cored, seeded, and thinly sliced

1 large onion, halved and
   thinly sliced

1 cup thinly sliced celery

1/4 teaspoon dried thyme, crumbled

Salt and freshly ground pepper

1/8 teaspoon crushed red pepper flakes

1 (28-ounce) can whole tomatoes,
   drained and coarsely chopped

1 teaspoon sugar

2 tablespoons fresh lemon juice

Hot cooked rice, for serving

1. On a cutting board, crush the garlic cloves with the flat side of a large knife. Coarsely chop the garlic, sprinkle with 1/4 teaspoon salt, and mash to a paste with the flat side of the knife. Scrape the mixture into a medium bowl. Add the oil, paprika, thyme, and red pepper flakes and mix well. Add the shrimp and toss to coat. Cover and refrigerate for up to 2 hours.

2. Make the creole sauce. In a large nonstick skillet, heat the oil over medium heat. Add the bell peppers, onion, celery, thyme, 1/4 teaspoon salt, 1/4 teaspoon pepper, and the red pepper flakes and cook, stirring, for 10 minutes, or until the vegetables are very tender. Add the tomatoes and sugar and bring to a simmer. Reduce the heat to low, cover, and simmer for 15 minutes. Remove from the heat and cover to keep warm.

3. Preheat the broiler and oil the broiler pan. Place the shrimp in a single layer on the prepared pan. Broil 3 to 5 inches from the heat source, turning once, for 4 to 5 minutes, until pink and just cooked through. Remove the pan from the heat, cover the shrimp loosely with foil, and set aside.

4. Return the sauce to a simmer. Add the lemon juice and shrimp, stirring to mix. To serve, spoon rice onto each plate and top with the shrimp and sauce.

SERVES 4 TO 6

lemon & chive Salmon cakes

fish cakes of all kinds have long been an American tradition, and it's easy to see why. They are a cinch to prepare and can be made with a variety of fish or shellfish, such as cod, crab, and shrimp. And most importantly, homemade fish cakes aren't overfilled with bread but include just enough to bind the ingredients. These cakes are great for casual entertaining, especially when served with tartar sauce, buttermilk biscuits, and your favorite cole slaw.

1 (15 1/2-ounce) can red salmon, drained

3/4 cup fresh bread crumbs

2 tablespoons finely chopped fresh parsley

1 tablespoon snipped fresh chives or
    2 teaspoons freeze-dried

1/2 teaspoon grated lemon zest

1 tablespoon fresh lemon juice, or to taste

1 large egg, lightly beaten

2 tablespoons milk

1 teaspoon Dijon mustard

Dash of Tabasco sauce, or to taste

1/2 cup fine dried bread crumbs

1/4 cup vegetable oil

1. Preheat the oven to 250°F.
2. In a medium bowl, stir together the salmon, fresh bread crumbs, parsley, chives, lemon zest and juice, egg, milk, mustard, and Tabasco until well combined. Shape the mixture into eight 2 1/2-inch rounds. Put the dried bread crumbs on a plate and coat each salmon cake thoroughly with the crumbs.
3. In a large nonstick skillet, heat 2 tablespoons of the oil over medium heat. Add half of the salmon cakes and cook for about 5 minutes on each side, or until golden brown. Transfer to an ovenproof platter and keep warm in the oven while you cook the remaining salmon cakes in the remaining 2 tablespoons oil.
4. Place two salmon cakes on each serving plate and pass the Tarragon Tartar Sauce separately. SERVES 4

TARRAGON TARTAR SAUCE

3/4 cup mayonnaise

2 small shallots, finely chopped

2 cornichons or gerkins,
    finely chopped

8 brine-cured green olives, pitted
    and chopped

2 teaspoons minced fresh tarragon leaves
    or 3/4 teaspoon dried, crumbled

1 1/2 teaspoons vinegar,
    preferably cider

Dash of Tabasco sauce, or to taste

In a small bowl, combine all the ingredients until well mixed. Serve immediately, or cover with plastic wrap and refrigerate until ready to use.

shrimp & Rice salad

Summer is the time for lazy entertaining, and this simple, refreshing salad is ideal. It is just as flavorful served at room temperature or slightly chilled. If you like, prepare it early in the day and store the salad, covered, in the refrigerator. Set it out about thirty minutes before serving, season with additional salt and pepper if necessary, and garnish. To add an exotic touch, use basmati or jasmine rice.

LEMON DRESSING

3/4 teaspoon grated lemon zest

2 tablespoons fresh lemon juice

1 teaspoon Dijon mustard

1 garlic clove, crushed with a
    garlic press

6 tablespoons olive oil

Salt and freshly ground pepper

1 cup long-grain white rice

1/8 teaspoon ground turmeric

1 bay leaf

2 teaspoons olive oil

1 pound medium shrimp, peeled
    and deveined

Salt and freshly ground pepper

1 cup frozen petite peas,
    thawed

1/4 cup chopped fresh parsley

Finely shredded romaine lettuce,
    for serving

3 plum tomatoes, seeded and
    finely chopped

Lemon wedges, for serving

1. In a small bowl, whisk together the lemon zest and juice, the mustard, and garlic. Add the oil in a slow stream, whisking until smooth and thickened. Season the mixture with salt and pepper. Set aside.

2. In a large pot of boiling salted water, cook the rice with the turmeric and bay leaf for 20 minutes, or until the rice is tender. Drain, discarding the bay leaf.

3. Transfer the hot rice to a large bowl and add the lemon dressing, tossing until well mixed. Set aside.

4. In a large nonstick skillet, heat the oil over medium-high heat. Add the shrimp and season with salt and pepper. Cook, stirring constantly, for 3 to 5 minutes, until the shrimp is just cooked through. Add the shrimp to the rice, along with the peas and parsley. Season with salt and pepper and toss until well mixed. Let the salad come to room temperature.

5. To serve, place the lettuce on a serving platter and spoon the shrimp and rice salad on top. Scatter the tomatoes on top of the salad and garnish with lemon wedges. **SERVES 4**

potluck ziti with Meatballs

t his easily transported one-dish entree is perfect for potluck parties and neighborhood get-togethers. The meatballs, seasoned the old-fashioned way with Parmesan cheese and herbs, are also delicious served as part of a hot buffet, over pasta, or in a hero sandwich.

MEATBALLS

1 tablespoon olive oil

1 medium onion, finely chopped

2 garlic cloves, crushed with a garlic press

1/2 teaspoon each dried basil and oregano

1 pound lean ground beef

1/2 cup Italian-seasoned dried bread crumbs

1/4 cup freshly grated Parmesan cheese

1/4 cup chopped fresh parsley

1 large egg

Salt and freshly ground pepper

8 ounces ziti

2 tablespoons olive oil

1 each red and green bell pepper, cored,
    seeded, cut into 1/2-inch strips, and
    halved crosswise

1 (26-ounce) jar marinara sauce

1 cup chicken broth or water

1 1/2 cups grated mozzarella cheese (6 ounces)

1. Preheat the oven to 425°F. Generously oil two jelly-roll pans.
2. In a small skillet, heat the oil over medium heat. Add the onion, garlic, basil, and oregano and cook, stirring, for 4 to 5 minutes, until the onion is softened. Remove from the heat.
3. In a large bowl, with your hands mix the beef, bread crumbs, Parmesan, parsley, egg, 1/2 teaspoon salt, and 1/4 teaspoon pepper until well combined. Stir in the onion mixture and mix well. Shape into about 4 dozen meatballs, using a scant tablespoon of the mixture for each. Arrange them in a single layer in the prepared pans.
4. Bake the meatballs for 10 to 12 minutes, until lightly browned and cooked through, shaking the pans occasionally to prevent them from sticking. Remove the meatballs from the oven, pour off the fat, and cover loosely with foil.
5. Reduce the oven temperature to 350°F. Oil a shallow 2 1/2- to 3-quart casserole.
6. Meanwhile, in a large pot of boiling salted water, cook the ziti for 7 to 8 minutes, until nearly al dente. Drain and toss with a little of the oil to prevent sticking.
7. Dry the pasta pot. Add the remaining oil and the bell peppers to the pot and cook over medium heat, stirring, for 10 minutes, or until the bell peppers are tender. Stir in the marinara sauce, broth, and meatballs and bring to a boil. Reduce the heat, cover, and simmer, stirring occasionally, for 10 minutes, or until heated through. Remove the pot from the heat and stir in the ziti. Spoon the mixture into the prepared casserole and sprinkle with the mozzarella. Bake for 15 to 20 minutes, until the sauce is bubbly and the cheese has melted. **SERVES 6 TO 8**

sicilian rigatoni & Sausage

main courses

Sicilians are famous for their tomato sauces, which are often flavored with oregano, basil, or a tasty piece of pork. The luscious results are invariably spooned over chicken, pasta, vegetables, or seafood. Fresh fennel, which has a licoricelike flavor, is added to this sauce to make it especially tasty. If you prefer sweet sausage over the spicy variety, use it instead—the result will be equally toothsome.

1/2 pound hot Italian sausage

2 tablespoons olive oil

1 fennel bulb, trimmed and finely
    chopped, feathery tops
    finely chopped and reserved

1 onion, finely chopped

1 celery stalk with leaves, finely chopped

2 garlic cloves, thinly sliced

5 medium tomatoes
    (about 2 pounds) chopped

1/4 cup chopped fresh basil, plus a few
    small sprigs for garnish

1/4 cup chopped fresh parsley

1 tablespoon tomato paste

Salt and freshly ground pepper

1 pound rigatoni or other large
    tube-shaped pasta

3/4 cup freshly grated Parmesan cheese,
    plus additional for serving

1. Prick each sausage several times with a fork. In a large skillet, heat 1 tablespoon of the oil over medium heat. Cook the sausage, turning often, for about 25 minutes, or until well browned and cooked through. With a slotted spoon, remove the sausage to a paper towel–lined plate.

2. Add the remaining 1 tablespoon oil to the skillet. Add the chopped fennel bulb, the onion, celery, and garlic and cook, stirring frequently, over medium-low heat for 20 minutes, or until the vegetables are very soft and lightly browned.

3. Add the tomatoes, basil, parsley, and tomato paste and season with salt and pepper. Cook, stirring occasionally, for 45 minutes, adding a little water if the sauce gets too thick. Press the sauce through a food mill set over a large saucepan.

4. Cut the sausage into 1/4-inch slices and add to the sauce. Cook over medium heat, stirring, for 5 minutes, or until the sauce is heated through.

5. Meanwhile, in a large pot of boiling salted water, cook the pasta until al dente. Drain the pasta, reserving 1/4 cup of the pasta water.

6. In a large serving bowl, toss the pasta with the Parmesan. Add the sauce and the reserved pasta water and toss again. Sprinkle the fennel tops over the pasta, garnish with the basil sprigs, and serve additional Parmesan alongside.

S E R V E S   4   T O   6

potato-onion Frittata

f rittata, an Italian-style omelette, is ideal for an impromptu lunch, Sunday brunch, or light supper. While in an omelette the ingredients are folded into the eggs, here they are cooked all together in a large skillet; the frittata is then cut into wedges and served. Use any of your favorite omelette ingredients—such as ham, cheese, tomato, or herbs—to personalize your frittata.

1 large all-purpose potato (about 10 ounces),
    peeled and cut into 1/2-inch cubes

2 tablespoons butter

2 red onions, cut into 1/4-inch slices

2 garlic cloves, minced

1 small zucchini, cut into 2- by 1/4-inch
    match sticks

2 tablespoons chopped fresh parsley

Salt and freshly ground pepper

8 large eggs

2 teaspoons balsamic vinegar

1. Preheat the oven to 350°F.

2. In a large saucepan, cover the potato with salted water and bring to a boil over high heat. Cook for 12 minutes, or until tender. Drain and set aside.

3. In a 10-inch nonstick ovenproof skillet, melt the butter over medium heat. Add the onions and garlic and cook, stirring occasionally, for 10 minutes, or until softened. Add the potato, zucchini, parsley, 1 teaspoon salt, and 1/4 teaspoon pepper and cook for 8 minutes, or until the zucchini is softened and most of the liquid has evaporated.

4. In a medium bowl, beat together the eggs and vinegar. Pour over the vegetables and stir until mixed. Cook over medium heat for about 3 minutes, or until the eggs just begin to set. Place the skillet in the oven and cook for about 10 minutes, or until the eggs are set. Let stand at room temperature, loosely covered, for 5 minutes.

5. To serve, with a spatula loosen the frittata from the skillet, invert onto a platter, and cut into six wedges.

S E R V E S   6

Sunday Night Supper

Potato-Onion Frittata

mixed greens salad

Apple Cider Vinaigrette
page 101

Crusty Rolls

Roasted Garlic Butter

Creamy Apricot Sorbet
page 159

Packaged
Shortbread Cookies

cornmeal pancakes with Cranberry compote

a special brunch entree, these beautiful pancakes are topped with a delectable, not-too-sweet maple-scented compote—a lovely alternative to plain maple syrup. The compote can be made up to one week ahead and rewarmed before serving, or it can be frozen for up to several months. Spoon any leftover compote over ice cream, or slather it over slices of toasted pound cake or coffee cake for a special breakfast treat.

CRANBERRY COMPOTE

1 (12-ounce) bag cranberries, picked
    over and rinsed

1 large apple, such as mutsu or Golden
    Delicious, peeled, halved, cored,
    and cut into 1/8-inch slices

1/2 cup sugar

1/4 teaspoon ground cinnamon

Pinch of ground allspice

3/4 cup water

1/2 cup maple syrup

PANCAKES

2 cups yellow cornmeal, preferably
    stone-ground

1/2 cup all-purpose flour

1 tablespoon sugar

2 teaspoons baking powder

1/2 teaspoon baking soda

1/2 teaspoon salt

1 1/2 cups buttermilk

1/2 cup water

1/4 cup vegetable oil

1 large egg

1. In a heavy medium nonreactive saucepan, combine all the ingredients for the compote and bring to a boil over high heat, stirring frequently. Reduce the heat to low and simmer, stirring occasionally, for 8 minutes, or until the cranberries pop and the apple slices soften. Set aside.

2. Preheat the oven to 200°F.

3. In a large bowl, whisk together the cornmeal, flour, sugar, baking powder, baking soda, and salt. In a medium bowl, beat the buttermilk, water, oil, and egg with a fork until blended. Add to the cornmeal mixture and mix with a wooden spoon until a smooth batter forms.

4. Lightly oil a griddle and heat over medium heat. For each pancake, pour a scant 1/4 cup of the batter onto the griddle. Cook for 2 to 3 minutes, until nicely browned on the bottom. Turn the pancakes and cook for about 2 minutes longer, or until browned on the second side. Transfer the pancakes to an oven-proof platter and keep warm in the oven while you cook the remaining pancakes.

5. To serve, transfer the cranberry compote to a bowl and serve alongside the pancakes. **SERVES 6**

brown sugar & Banana waffles

t he secret to really good waffles is to cook them long enough: It's so easy to get impatient and take them out of the waffle iron before they're deep golden brown and crisp. Like most waffles, these taste best hot and fresh, but if you're making a large batch, keep them hot by placing them directly on the racks of a 250°F oven. (They can be made ahead and frozen between sheets of waxed paper.) Bacon is the perfect partner for these slightly sweet waffles.

powder, baking soda, and salt. In a medium bowl, whisk together the buttermilk, brown sugar, eggs, and vanilla. Pour into the cornmeal mixture and whisk just until combined. Stir in the banana slices and melted butter.

3. Lightly butter or oil the waffle iron. Pour a generous 1/2 cup batter (or the amount recommended by the waffle iron's manufacturer) onto the hot waffle iron. With a wooden spoon, spread the batter to the edges of the grids. Close the lid and bake until the waffle is dark brown and crisp. Place the waffle directly on an oven rack and continue making waffles. Serve the waffles accompanied by maple syrup.

MAKES EIGHT 7-INCH WAFFLES

1 1/4 cups all-purpose flour

3/4 cup yellow cornmeal, preferably
   stone-ground

2 teaspoons baking powder

1/2 teaspoon baking soda

1/4 teaspoon salt

2 cups buttermilk

1/2 cup packed brown sugar

2 large eggs

1/2 teaspoon vanilla extract

1 large ripe banana, cut into
   1/4-inch slices

1/4 cup (1/2 stick) unsalted butter,
   melted

Heated maple syrup, for serving

1. Preheat a waffle iron.

2. In a large bowl, whisk together the flour, cornmeal, baking

main courses

Sunday Brunch

Sweet & Spicy Nuts
page 13

smoked salmon-
cream cheese dip and crackers

Brown Sugar
& Banana Waffles

Warm Maple Syrup

Hickory-Smoked Bacon

Double Pear Crisp
page 134

Chapter Four

Side dishes & Salads

roasted asparagus with Lemon & pine nuts

f resh asparagus heralds the beginning of spring, and there are countless ways to enjoy this versatile green vegetable when it is plentiful in the market. Serve cold cooked asparagus dressed with an anchovy vinaigrette as part of an antipasto spread, as a silken-textured soup garnished with steamed asparagus tips for an elegant first course, or include as part of a chopped vegetable salad.

2 tablespoons pine nuts or slivered almonds

1 1/2 pounds asparagus, tough ends trimmed

2 tablespoons extra-virgin olive oil

1 tablespoon loosely packed slivered lemon zest

Kosher salt

Freshly ground pepper

Lemon wedges, for garnish

side dishes & salads

1. Preheat the oven to 425°F. Oil a 13- x 9-inch baking dish.

2. In a small skillet, toast the nuts, shaking the pan several times, for 12 minutes, or until golden. Transfer the nuts to a small dish and set aside.

3. Put the asparagus into the prepared baking dish. Sprinkle with the oil, lemon zest, and 1/2 teaspoon Kosher salt, turning the asparagus until evenly coated with the oil. Roast the asparagus, turning them a few times, for 15 to 20 minutes, or until tender.

4. Season the asparagus with pepper and transfer to a serving platter. Sprinkle the asparagus with the pine nuts, garnish with the lemon wedges, and serve hot or at room temperature.

SERVES 4 TO 6

shiitake mushroom &
Barley pilaf

b arley, one of the oldest cultivated grains, has an earthy, nutty flavor that is the ideal partner for shiitake mushrooms in this hearty pilaf. Serve with any meat dish that contains gravy, sauce, or lots of pan juices—you can spoon some over the barley. If you're not yet a barley lover, this recipe is guaranteed to convert you.

3 cups water

1 cup quick-cooking barley

1/4 pound white mushrooms, sliced

1 celery stalk with leaves, stalks cut into

1/4-inch dice, leaves chopped

1/4 cup finely chopped fresh parsley

1 scallion, finely chopped

Salt and freshly ground pepper

1. In a medium saucepan, bring 3 cups of salted water to a boil over high heat. Stir in the barley, mushrooms, and celery and return to a boil. Reduce the heat to low. Cover and simmer, stirring occasionally, for 10 to 12 minutes, until the barley is tender; drain.

2. To serve, transfer the barley mixture to a serving bowl, stir in the parsley and scallion, and season with salt and pepper. **S E R V E S   4**

broccoli with
Orange butter

h ere, orange enlivens broccoli, turning it into a delicious and very unusual vegetable side dish.

1 medium bunch broccoli, separated into

2-inch florets

2 navel oranges

2 tablespoons unsalted butter

2 shallots, finely chopped

1 small garlic clove, thinly sliced

Salt

Ground red pepper

1. In a large pot of boiling salted water, cook the broccoli for 4 minutes, or until crisp-tender. Drain and let the broccoli dry on paper towels.

2. With a small knife, peel the oranges, making sure to remove all the white pith. Remove the orange sections by cutting along the membranes, letting the sections and juice fall into a small bowl.

3. In a large skillet, melt the butter over medium heat. Add the shallots and garlic and cook, stirring, for 2 minutes, or until softened. Add the broccoli and season with salt and red pepper. Cook, stirring, for 2 minutes. Remove the skillet from the heat and gently stir in the orange sections and juice. Transfer to a bowl and serve. **S E R V E S   4   T O   6**

orange & honey-Glazed carrots

Spring carrots or packaged baby-cut carrots, readily available in supermarkets, are best for this recipe.

I pound baby carrots

2 tablespoons butter

I garlic clove, halved

2 tablespoons honey

I/8 teaspoon grated orange zest

Salt and freshly ground pepper

I tablespoon snipped fresh chives

1. In a large saucepan of boiling salted water, cook the carrots for 5 to 7 minutes, until tender. Drain.

2. In a large skillet, melt the butter over medium heat. Add the garlic and cook, stirring, for 2 minutes. Remove the garlic and discard. Add the honey, stirring to blend. Increase the heat to medium-high and add the carrots, orange zest, 1/4 teaspoon salt, and 1/8 teaspoon pepper. Cook, stirring occasionally, for 10 minutes, or until the carrots begin to brown.

3. To serve, transfer the carrots to a bowl and sprinkle with the chives. **SERVES 4**

cauliflower with Parmesan crumbs

side dishes & salads

here the natural sweetness of the cauliflower plays against the saltiness of the Parmesan with much success.

I large head cauliflower, separated into florets

2 tablespoons extra-virgin olive oil

3 garlic cloves, minced

I/4 teaspoon dried oregano, crumbled

Salt

I/4 teaspoon crushed red pepper flakes

I/4 cup plain dried bread crumbs

I/4 cup freshly grated Parmesan cheese

I/4 cup chopped fresh parsley

1. In a large skillet or saucepan, bring 1/2 inch of salted water to a boil over high heat. Add the cauliflower and cook, stirring occasionally, for 6 to 8 minutes, until tender. Drain, return the cauliflower to the pan, and cover to keep warm.

2. In a medium skillet, put the oil, garlic, oregano, 1/4 teaspoon salt, and the red pepper flakes. Cook over medium-low heat, stirring often, for 3 to 4 minutes, until the garlic begins to sizzle. Stir in the bread crumbs, increase the heat to medium, and cook, stirring frequently, for 3 to 4 minutes, until the crumbs are lightly toasted.

3. Transfer the cauliflower to a serving bowl, add the crumb mixture, Parmesan, and parsley and toss until the cauliflower is evenly coated. Serve hot.

SERVES 4 TO 6

grilled portobellos with fresh Thyme

Serve these meaty mushrooms over a juicy steak, alongside blue-cheese burgers, or tucked into your favorite grilled vegetable and mozzarella sandwich.

2 tablespoons extra-virgin olive oil

1 1/2 tablespoons fresh lemon juice

1 garlic clove, crushed with a
   garlic press

1 1/2 teaspoons chopped fresh thyme or
   1/2 teaspoon dried

Salt and freshly ground pepper

2 (6-ounce) packages sliced portobellos

1. In a small jar, put the oil, lemon juice, garlic, thyme, 1/2 teaspoon salt, and 1/4 teaspoon pepper. Cover and shake.

2. Arrange half of the mushroom slices in a shallow baking dish. Pour half the dressing over, then repeat with the remaining mushrooms and dressing, making sure the mushrooms are coated with the marinade. Cover and marinate for at least 1 hour or up to 3 hours, turning the mushrooms once.

3. Preheat the grill to medium-high and oil the grill.

4. Turn the mushroom slices once more to coat with the marinade, then arrange in a single layer on the grill rack. Cover and grill, turning once, for 10 to 12 minutes, until the mushrooms are well browned and tender. Serve hot.

SERVES 4 TO 6

sauteed mushrooms with Peas & parsley

Peas and mushrooms are a delicate and delicious flavor combination. This easy-to-prepare recipe is sure to become a year-round favorite. Serve hot alongside a favorite main dish, such as roast beef or baked chicken, or simply spoon over crisp breaded fish fillets for a weeknight treat.

2 tablespoons butter

1/2 pound white mushrooms,
   sliced

Salt and freshly ground pepper

1 (10-ounce) package frozen petite
   peas, thawed

2 teaspoons finely chopped fresh parsley

1. In a large nonstick skillet, melt the butter over medium heat. Add the mushrooms, 1/4 teaspoon salt, and 1/8 teaspoon pepper and cook, stirring, for 6 minutes, or until most of the mushroom liquid has evaporated.

2. Add the peas and parsley and cook, stirring, for 4 minutes, or until heated through. Serve hot.

SERVES 4

baked double cheese & Macaroni

side dishes
& salads

Whether you grew up on Kraft Macaroni and Cheese™ or a favorite family recipe, this double-cheese version will win you over. Under the crispy crumb topping is a robust, creamy blend of ingredients. Here, scallions replace onions, adding just the right amount of zing. This is a great make-ahead dish—simply reheat in the oven or microwave.

1/4 cup (1/2 stick) butter

1/3 cup all-purpose flour

3 cups milk

10 ounces extra-sharp cheddar cheese,
   grated (2 1/2 cups)

3/4 cup freshly grated Parmesan cheese

1/2 cup thinly sliced scallions

Salt and freshly ground pepper

12 ounces elbow macaroni, cooked according
   to package directions and drained

1 cup fresh bread crumbs (about 3 slices
   firm-textured white bread)

1. Preheat the oven to 350°F. Butter a 2-quart baking dish.
2. In a large heavy saucepan, melt 3 tablespoons of the butter over medium heat. Stir in the flour and cook, whisking, for 1 minute. Remove from the heat and whisk in the milk.
3. Whisk the sauce well and place over medium heat. Cook, stirring often, until the sauce boils and thickens. Reduce the heat to low and cook, stirring often, for 5 minutes, to cook the flour. Add the cheddar, Parmesan, scallions, 3/4 teaspoon salt, and 1/4 teaspoon pepper, or to taste, stirring until the cheeses have melted. Fold in the cooked macaroni.
4. Remove from the heat.
5. Scrape the macaroni mixture into the prepared baking dish.
6. In a medium skillet, melt the remaining 1 tablespoon butter over medium heat. Add the bread crumbs and cook, stirring, for 3 minutes, or until lightly toasted. Sprinkle evenly over the macaroni and cheese.
7. Bake for 25 to 30 minutes, until bubbly and lightly browned on top. S E R V E S 4 T O 6

side dishes
& salads

garlic mashed Potato casserole

 otato casseroles don't get any better than this. The inside puffs up light and fluffy, and the Parmesan topping gets brown and crusty. If you like, put the entire dish together and set aside in the refrigerator until 45 minutes before serving; then simply pop it into the oven. Serve with roasted pork, grilled chicken, or mustard-broiled lamb chops.

2 pounds baking potatoes, peeled and cut

into large chunks

1/4 cup thinly sliced garlic

1 cup chicken broth

1/2 cup regular or light sour cream

2 tablespoons butter

Salt and freshly ground pepper

1/4 cup thinly sliced scallions

1/2 cup freshly grated Parmesan cheese

1 tablespoon olive oil, preferably extra-virgin

1. Put the potatoes, garlic, broth, and 2 cups water into a large pot. Cover and bring the liquid to a boil over high heat. Reduce the heat to medium-low and simmer for about 15 minutes, or until the potatoes are very tender.

2. Preheat the oven to 400°F. Butter a 2-quart baking dish.

3. Set aside 3/4 cup of the potato water. Drain the potatoes and garlic. Return them to the pot and heat over medium heat, stirring, for 1 to 2 minutes, until the potatoes are dry.

4. Mash the potatoes, adding a little of the reserved potato water if necessary. With a wooden spoon, beat in the sour cream, butter, 1/2 teaspoon salt, 1/2 teaspoon pepper, and the remaining potato water, beating until the potatoes are very soft and fluffy. Gently stir in 3 tablespoons of the scallions.

5. Spoon the potatoes into the prepared dish. Sprinkle with the Parmesan and drizzle with the oil. Bake for about 30 minutes, or until the top is golden and puffed. Sprinkle with the remaining 1 tablespoon scallions and serve.

SERVES 4 TO 6

Sunday Afternoon Dinner

Cucumber, Beet and
Scallion Salad
page 104

Oven-Fried Lemon Chicken
page 37

Garlic Mashed Potato Casserole

Whole Green Beans with
Toasted Pecans

Double Pear Crisp
page 134

oven-roasted Potatoes & carrots

Warm your insides with this perfect cold-weather food. The vegetables caramelize in the oven, gaining an intense sweetness.

1 1/4 pounds small red potatoes
   (about 8), quartered

4 medium carrots, halved lengthwise
   and then crosswise

6 garlic cloves, unpeeled, lightly smashed

Salt and freshly ground pepper

1 tablespoon extra-virgin olive oil

1. Preheat the oven to 425°F. Oil a 2-quart baking dish.

2. Put the potatoes, carrots, garlic, 1/4 teaspoon salt, 1/4 teaspoon pepper, and the oil into the prepared baking dish and toss until well mixed. Cover with a sheet of foil. Roast the vegetables for 1 hour.

3. Remove the foil and gently toss the vegetables. Bake for 20 to 30 minutes longer, until the potatoes and carrots are lightly browned and very tender. **SERVES 4 TO 6**

sour cream Mashed potatoes

side dishes & salads

these mashed potatoes contain the best part of baked potatoes—the toppings. Sour cream and chives add flavor to any good baking potato, such as russet or Idaho. These varieties develop a dry, fluffy texture when cooked, which makes them ideal for mashing. If you would like to keep the calories down, substitute reduced-fat sour cream.

3 pounds all-purpose potatoes,
   peeled and cut into
   3/4-inch chunks

Salt and freshly ground pepper

1 (8-ounce) container sour cream

3 tablespoons snipped fresh chives

1. In a large saucepan, cover the potatoes with salted water and bring to a boil over high heat. Reduce the heat to low. Cover and simmer for 15 minutes, or until the potatoes are tender when pierced with a fork.

2. Drain the potatoes and return them to the pot. Heat over high heat, shaking the pan, for about 30 seconds, or until any liquid has evaporated. Remove from the heat.

3. Mash the potatoes until smooth and season with 1 teaspoon salt and 1/4 teaspoon pepper. Add the sour cream and chives and stir until well combined. Transfer the potatoes to a bowl and serve. **SERVES 8**

sauteed spinach with Garlic

fabulous and garlicky, this heavenly side dish is also good spooned onto a baked potato and topped with a bit of sour cream for a quick late-night supper. If you're an insatiable spinach lover, you just might need to triple the recipe!

2 large bunches spinach (about 2 pounds),
    tough stems removed and well rinsed, or
    2 (10-ounce) bags spinach
2 tablespoons extra-virgin olive oil
8 garlic cloves, lightly smashed
Salt and freshly ground pepper

1. In a large heavy skillet, bring 1/4 inch of salted water to a boil over high heat. Add the spinach in batches and then cook, tossing frequently, for 1 minute, or until just wilted. Drain the spinach and set aside until cool enough to handle. Using your hands, squeeze out the excess water from the spinach, then coarsely chop it.

2. Wipe out the skillet with paper towels. Add the oil and garlic and cook over medium heat, stirring constantly, for about 4 minutes, or until the garlic is lightly golden brown.

3. Add the spinach to the skillet and cook until well coated with the garlic oil and heated through. Season to taste with salt and pepper and serve. **SERVES 4**

herbed squash with Onion & garlic

make this squash dish, delicately flavored with marjoram, when you long for a new way to cook an overly generous crop of homegrown squash.

2 small zucchini (about 5 ounces each)
2 summer squash (about 5 ounces each),
2 tablespoons butter
1 large onion, halved and thinly sliced
3 garlic cloves, minced
1/2 teaspoon dried marjoram, crumbled
Salt and freshly ground pepper
2 tablespoons chopped fresh parsley

1. In a food processor fitted with the slicing blade, slice the zucchini and summer squash in batches. Set aside.

2. In a large nonstick skillet, melt the butter over medium heat. Add the onion, garlic, and marjoram and cook, stirring often, for about 5 minutes, or until tender.

3. Stir in the zucchini, summer squash, 1/2 teaspoon salt, and 1/8 teaspoon pepper, and toss to mix. Cook, stirring, for 2 minutes, or until the squash begins to give off some liquid. Reduce the heat to medium-low. Cover and cook, stirring occasionally, for 5 to 7 minutes, until the squash is very tender. Remove from the heat.

4. Drain any liquid from the pan, stir in the parsley, and season with salt and pepper if necessary. Transfer to a bowl and serve. **SERVES 4 TO 6**

minted squash with Peas & tomatoes

r ipe tomatoes lend a fresh tang, while a combination of fresh and dried herbs gives new life to the subtle flavors of zucchini, petite peas, and summer squash.

1 tablespoon extra-virgin olive oil

1 medium onion, halved and thinly sliced

1/4 teaspoon dried thyme, crumbled

1/2 teaspoon sugar

Salt and freshly ground pepper

1 each medium zucchini and summer squash,
   halved and cut into 1/4-inch slices

3 small tomatoes, cut into 1/2-inch
   wedges

1 cup frozen petite peas

2 tablespoons water

2 tablespoons coarsely chopped fresh mint

1. In a large skillet, heat the oil over medium heat. Add the onion, thyme, sugar, 1/2 teaspoon salt, and 1/4 teaspoon pepper, and cook, stirring, for 4 to 6 minutes, until the onion is softened.

2. Add the zucchini and summer squash. Cook, stirring, for 5 to 6 minutes, until the squash is nearly tender. Stir in the tomatoes. Cover and cook, stirring, for 3 minutes longer.

3. Add the peas and water. Cover and cook for 3 minutes, just until the peas are heated through. Transfer to a bowl, toss in the mint, and serve. **SERVES 4 TO 6**

side dishes & salads

brown sugar-baked Acorn squash

t he brown sugar caramelizes while the acorn squash bakes, bringing out the vegetable's natural sweetness. Bacon adds an enticing smokiness that completes the dish.

1 large acorn squash (about 2 1/4 pounds),
   cut into 8 wedges and seeded

Salt and freshly ground pepper

2 tablespoons packed brown sugar

2 slices bacon, cut into 1/2-inch strips

1 tablespoon finely
   chopped fresh parsley

1. Preheat the oven to 400°F.

2. Season the squash with 1/4 teaspoon salt and 1/8 teaspoon pepper. Arrange cut side down in a 13- x 9-inch baking dish. Cover with foil and bake for 35 minutes, or until the squash is tender when pierced with a fork.

3. Arrange the squash wedges skin side down, sprinkle with the sugar, and bake, uncovered, for 20 minutes longer, or until the squash browns around the edges.

4. In a large skillet, cook the bacon until crisp and browned. With a slotted spoon, transfer the bacon to a paper towel–lined plate.

5. To serve, arrange the squash wedges on a small platter, and sprinkle with the bacon and parsley. **SERVES 4**

crisp cornmeal-Fried tomatoes

 his is luscious backyard picnic food when accompanied by buttermilk-fried chicken, creamy potato salad, and freshly made cole slaw.

I cup yellow cornmeal, preferably
    stone-ground
1/2 cup freshly grated
    Parmesan cheese
1/3 cup all-purpose flour
2 large eggs
4 medium "green or pink"
    (slightly underripe) tomatoes,
    cut into 1/2-inch slices
Salt and freshly ground pepper
Vegetable oil, for frying

1. Set out two jelly-roll pans. Line one pan with waxed paper and the other with paper towels.
2. In a pie plate, mix the cornmeal, Parmesan, and flour. In another pie plate, beat the eggs with a fork until frothy.
3. Sprinkle the tomatoes with 1/2 teaspoon salt and 1/8 teaspoon pepper. Dip the tomatoes in the beaten egg and then dredge in the cornmeal mixture, making sure each slice is evenly coated on both sides and gently tapping off the excess crumbs. Place the tomatoes on the waxed paper–lined pan, placing a sheet of waxed paper between the layers.
4. In a large nonstick or cast-iron skillet, heat 1/8 inch of oil over medium-high heat until hot. Fry the tomatoes in batches, for 3 to 4 minutes, until golden brown on the bottom. Turn and cook for 2 to 3 minutes longer, until golden brown and crisp on both sides, adding additional oil if necessary. Drain the tomatoes on the paper towels, then transfer to a platter and serve. **SERVES 4**

scalloped summer Tomatoes

ake advantage of summer's tomato bounty with this old-fashioned favorite. Use the ripest, tangiest tomatoes you can find, or try a mix of red and yellow tomatoes. If you wish, vary the flavorings: Substitute dried oregano for the marjoram, or sprinkle the tomatoes with fresh basil. Scalloped tomatoes are equally good fresh from the oven or shredded and served at room temperature.

5 large tomatoes (about 2 1/2 pounds)

2 teaspoons sugar

1/2 teaspoon dried marjoram, crumbled

Salt and freshly ground pepper

2 tablespoons olive oil, preferably

    extra-virgin

2 medium onions, coarsely chopped

2 garlic cloves, minced

1 cup fresh bread crumbs

    (about 3 slices firm-textured

    white bread)

1. Preheat the oven to 375°F. Butter a 2-quart baking dish.

2. Bring a large saucepan of water to a boil. Using a small knife, cut a small X in the bottom of each tomato. In two batches, put the tomatoes into the boiling water and blanch for about 30 seconds. Using a slotted spoon, remove the tomatoes and cool briefly under cold running water. Peel and cut into 3/4-inch slices.

3. In a small dish, mix the sugar, marjoram, 3/4 teaspoon salt, and 1/2 teaspoon pepper.

4. In a medium skillet, heat 1 tablespoon of the oil over medium heat. Add the onions and garlic and cook, stirring, for about 4 minutes, or until the onions begin to soften and turn golden. Stir in 1 teaspoon of the marjoram mixture and cook, stirring, for 30 seconds longer. Remove from the heat.

5. Place half of the tomatoes in the prepared dish, overlapping the slices as needed. Sprinkle with half of the remaining marjoram mixture. Spoon half the onions over the tomatoes and sprinkle with half of the bread crumbs. Repeat the layers, drizzling the remaining 1 tablespoon oil on top.

6. Bake for 40 to 45 minutes, until the juices are bubbly and the crumbs are lightly browned.

SERVES 4 TO 6

parmesan-glazed Tomatoes

this is a great way to use up tomatoes that aren't perfectly ripe—the combination of baking and broiling greatly intensifies their flavor and gives them an enticing glaze.

3 medium tomatoes, cut into 3/4-inch slices

3 tablespoons mayonnaise

3 tablespoons freshly grated Parmesan cheese

1 teaspoon Dijon mustard

2 tablespoons finely chopped fresh parsley

2 teaspoons finely snipped fresh or

   freeze-dried chives

Salt and freshly ground pepper

1. Preheat the oven to 400°F.

2. Arrange the tomatoes in a nonreactive baking pan or on a broiler pan large enough to hold them in a single layer.

3. In a small bowl, combine the mayonnaise, 2 tablespoons of the Parmesan, the mustard, 1 tablespoon of the parsley, and the chives. Season with salt and pepper to taste. Spread the mayonnaise mixture on the tomatoes and sprinkle with the remaining 1 tablespoon Parmesan.

4. Bake the tomatoes for 10 minutes, or until heated through.

5. Turn on the broiler. Broil the tomatoes 4 to 6 inches from the heat source for about 2 minutes, or until the topping is golden and bubbly. Sprinkle with remaining 1 tablespoon parsley and serve hot. **SERVES 6**

monterey jack & Jalapeño corn bread

bake this decadent corn bread in a cast-iron skillet for the crispiest top and most tender crumb. Cut the corn bread into very small portions and serve on a warm summer's night with a pitcher of margaritas or with Mexican beer, or offer alongside Chunky Beef Chili (page 54).

1 1/4 cups yellow cornmeal, preferably stoneground

1/2 cup all-purpose flour

1 tablespoon sugar

2 1/2 teaspoons baking powder

1/2 teaspoon baking soda

1/2 teaspoon salt

1/4 teaspoon freshly ground pepper

1 cup sour cream

3 large eggs

1/4 cup (1/2 stick) unsalted butter,
  melted and cooled

1 1/2 cups frozen or drained canned
  corn kernels

1 tablespoon minced seeded pickled jalapeño chiles

3/4 cup grated Monterey Jack cheese

1. Preheat the oven to 375°F. Generously butter a 10- to 11-inch cast-iron skillet.

2. In a large bowl, combine the cornmeal, flour, sugar, baking powder, baking soda, salt, and pepper.

3. In a medium bowl, whisk the sour cream, eggs, and butter until well blended. Stir in the corn, jalapeños, and cheese.

4. Add the sour cream mixture to the cornmeal mixture, stirring just until mixed. Spoon the batter in the prepared pan, spreading it evenly.

5. Bake for 25 to 30 minutes, until lightly browned on top and a wooden pick inserted into the center comes out clean. Transfer the pan to a wire rack and let the corn bread cool slightly before serving. **SERVES 8**

**side dishes
& salads**

buttermilk-scallion Drop biscuits

drop biscuits are even easier to make than rolled biscuits—the dough is so moist that it can be dropped by tablespoonfuls onto a baking sheet. Fresh from the oven, the biscuits look like large, savory scones. They make tasty little sandwich snacks when halved and filled with thinly sliced turkey, Brie cheese, and slivered sun-dried tomatoes.

2 cups all-purpose flour

2 teaspoons baking powder

1/4 teaspoon baking soda

1/2 teaspoon dried thyme, crumbled

1/4 teaspoon dried sage, crumbled

1/2 teaspoon salt

1/4 teaspoon coarsely ground pepper

1 cup buttermilk

3 tablespoons olive oil

1/4 cup thinly sliced scallions (green part only)

1. Preheat the oven to 425°F. Grease a heavy baking sheet.
2. In a large bowl, combine the flour, baking powder, baking soda, thyme, sage, salt, and pepper.
3. In a small bowl, combine the buttermilk, oil, and scallions. Pour into the flour mixture and stir just until a soft dough forms.
4. Drop the dough by heaping tablespoonfuls 1 1/2 inches apart on the prepared baking sheet.
5. Bake for 11 to 13 minutes, until the biscuits are lightly browned on top. Serve warm.

MAKES ABOUT ONE DOZEN

Fireside Supper

❧

Sweet n' Spicy Nuts
page 13

Mixed Green Salad
Creamy Buttermilk Dressing
page 101

Mom's Best Beef Stew
page 51

Buttermilk-Scallion
Drop Biscuits

Farmhouse Walnut Pie
page 127

Vinaigrettes & Dressings

Just as there are many kinds of salads, there are many kinds of vinaigrettes. Some are creamy and smooth, some are thick and chunky, still others are enticingly spicy or deliciously sweet. There are dressings just made for spooning over a plate of fresh fruit, a crisp green salad, or even warm grilled vegetables. Here are a few vinaigrettes we think are very special and very delicious.

fresh lemon and oregano vinaigrette

In a medium bowl, combine the zest of 1 lemon (removed with a vegetable peeler); the juice of 2 lemons; 1 small shallot, finely minced; 1 tablespoon chopped fresh parsley; 1 teaspoon Dijon mustard; 1/2 teaspoon dried oregano; and 1/2 teaspoon sugar. Slowly pour in 1 cup extra-virgin olive oil, whisking constantly. Season with salt and freshly ground pepper. Refrigerate until ready to use.

MAKES 1 1/2 CUPS

honey mustard dressing

In a medium bowl, whisk together 1/4 cup honey mustard; 1 tablespoon grainy mustard; 2 tablespoons white wine vinegar; and 1 small onion, finely minced. Slowly pour in 1 cup extra-virgin olive oil, whisking constantly. Season with salt and freshly ground pepper. Refrigerate until ready to use.

MAKES ABOUT 1 1/2 CUPS

apple cider vinaigrette

In a medium bowl, combine 1/2 cup cider vinegar; 1 small shallot, minced;

1 tablespoon Dijon mustard; 1 tablespoon chopped fresh tarragon or 1/4 teaspoon dried tarragon;

1/2 teaspoon salt; and 1 teaspoon freshly ground pepper.

Slowly pour in 1 cup extra-virgin olive oil, whisking constantly.

MAKES ABOUT 1 1/2 CUPS

spicy tomato vinaigrette

In a medium bowl, combine 1 cup tomato juice; 1/3 cup fresh lemon juice; 2 teaspoons Worcestershire sauce;

and 1/2 teaspoon celery salt. Add 1/2 cup mild olive oil

in a slow steady stream, whisking constantly. Season with salt,

freshly ground pepper, and hot pepper sauce. Refrigerate until ready to use.

MAKES ABOUT 2 CUPS

creamy buttermilk dressing

In a medium bowl, combine 1 cup mayonnaise; 1 cup buttermilk; 1 garlic clove, minced; 2 tablespoons minced

scallion (green part only); 1 tablespoon chopped fresh parsley; and 1/2 teaspoon paprika, stirring until well blended.

Season with salt and freshly ground pepper. Refrigerate until ready to use.

MAKES 2 CUPS

roasted garlic and red wine vinaigrette

In a medium bowl, combine 2 tablespoons roasted garlic; 2 tablespoons chopped fresh thyme or 1/2 teaspoon

dried thyme; 1 tablespoon chopped fresh parsley; and 1/4 cup red wine vinegar. Slowly pour in 1 cup extra-virgin

olive oil, whisking constantly. Season with salt and freshly ground pepper. Refrigerate until ready to use.

MAKES ABOUT 1 1/2 CUPS

farmers' market Green beans

When basil is full and fragrant, green beans are small and tender, and the first ripe tomatoes appear in the market, it is time to make this robust salad.

1 pound green beans, halved

1 tablespoon extra-virgin olive oil

1 cup thinly sliced red onions

2 garlic cloves, very thinly sliced

One 12-ounce basket cherry tomatoes, halved

Salt and freshly ground pepper

1/4 cup shredded fresh basil leaves

1. In a large skillet, bring 1/2 inch of water to a boil over high heat. Add a large pinch of salt and the green beans and boil uncovered, stirring often, for about 10 minutes, or until tender. Drain. Wipe out the skillet with paper towels.

2. Heat the oil in the same skillet over medium heat. Add the onions and garlic and cook, stirring, for about 5 minutes, or until the onions are tender and lightly browned. Stir in the cherry tomatoes and cook, stirring, for 2 to 3 minutes, until they begin to collapse and give up their juices.

3. Add the green beans, 1/2 teaspoon salt, and 1/8 teaspoon pepper and cook until the beans are heated through. Stir in the basil and spoon into a bowl. Serve hot or at room temperature.

SERVES 4 TO 6

confetti Cole slaw

If crisp cole slaw is your preference, toss this together about thirty minutes before serving. But if wilted slaw is more to your liking, prepare it up to one day ahead, but be sure to toss it several times while it rests.

1/2 cup sour cream

2 teaspoons cider vinegar

1 1/2 cups finely shredded red cabbage

1 cup finely shredded green cabbage

1/2 cup grated carrots

3/4 cup thinly sliced bell peppers, preferably a combination of yellow and red

2 tablespoons snipped fresh chives

Salt and freshly ground pepper

1. In a small bowl, combine the sour cream and vinegar.

2. In a large bowl, combine the red and green cabbages, the carrots, bell peppers, and chives. Add the sour cream mixture and toss until well mixed. Season with salt and pepper, transfer to a bowl, and serve. **SERVES 4**

cucumber, beet & Scallion salad

side dishes
& salads

1 bunch beets (about 1 3/4 pounds), tops
  trimmed to 1 inch and scrubbed

2 large cucumbers, peeled, halved, seeded,
  and cut into 1/4-inch slices

Kosher salt

1/2 cup light or regular sour cream

1/2 cup thinly sliced scallions

2 tablespoons red wine vinegar

1 tablespoon prepared white horseradish

1 tablespoon sugar

Salt and freshly ground pepper

1. Preheat the oven to 400°F.

2. Wrap each beet in a sheet of foil. Bake for 1 to 1 1/2 hours, until the beets are easily pierced with a small knife. Unwrap.

3. Meanwhile, in a medium bowl, combine the cucumbers and 1 teaspoon Kosher salt; cover with plastic wrap. Set a plate on top, weight with a heavy can, and refrigerate for about 1 hour. Rinse the cucumbers, drain, and put into a medium bowl.

4. When the beets are cool enough to handle, peel, quarter, and cut crosswise into 1/4-inch slices. Add to the cucumbers.

5. In a small bowl, combine the sour cream, scallions, vinegar, horseradish, sugar, 1/4 teaspoon salt, and 1/4 teaspoon pepper. Add to the beet mixture and toss until mixed. Spoon into a bowl and serve at room temperature or slightly chilled.

SERVES 4 TO 6

grilled Vegetable salad

t his eye-catching salad has all the zesty flavors of an antipasto. A rainbowlike assortment of grilled vegetables is livened up with a piquant dressing of Kalamata olives and peperoncini (hot-sweet pickled peppers). Heap the vegetables onto a platter and surround with grilled shrimp, grilled thickly sliced country bread, and a generous wedge of Parmesan cheese.

1/4 cup olive oil

2 garlic cloves, crushed with a
   garlic press

Salt and coarsely ground pepper

1 slender medium eggplant (about
   1 pound), cut into 3/4-inch slices,
   large slices halved

2 medium zucchini, cut lengthwise into
   1/4-inch slices

2 large red bell peppers, cored, quartered,
   and seeded

1 large red onion, cut into 1/2-inch slices

OLIVE DRESSING

1 large shallot, minced

3 tablespoons extra-virgin olive oil

1 tablespoon balsamic vinegar

1 tablespoon red wine vinegar

12 Kalamata olives, pitted and
   coarsely chopped

6 peperoncini, stemmed, seeded,
   and coarsely chopped

Salt and freshly ground pepper

1. Preheat the grill to medium and brush with oil.

2. In a small jar, put the oil, garlic, 1 teaspoon salt, and 1/2 teaspoon coarsely ground pepper. Cover the jar and shake until well blended.

3. Put the eggplant, zucchini, bell peppers, and onion in a large roasting pan or on a baking sheet, keeping each vegetable separate. Pour the garlic-oil mixture over the vegetables and toss to coat well (still keeping the vegetables separate since they have different cooking times).

4. Grill the vegetables, covered, in batches if necessary, turning them several times, for 15 to 25 minutes, until very tender and lightly charred. Transfer the vegetables to a serving bowl and cool to room temperature.

5. Make the olive dressing. In a medium bowl, whisk together the shallot, oil, and balsamic and red wine vinegars until well mixed. Stir in the olives, peperoncini, 1/8 teaspoon salt, and 1/8 teaspoon pepper. Spoon the dressing over the vegetables and serve. **SERVES 6**

fresh corn &
Tomato succotash

Sweet summer corn, scarlet chunks of tomato, and a splash of vinegar make this succotash a perennial favorite. To enjoy this during the winter when vegetables aren't at their flavorful best, substitute frozen corn and cherry tomatoes.

1 (10-ounce) package frozen baby lima beans

2 tablespoons vegetable oil

3/4 cup each finely chopped red onion
   and celery

1 garlic clove, minced

1 large tomato, seeded and chopped

1/2 cup fresh corn kernels

1 tablespoon chopped fresh parsley

1 tablespoon cider vinegar

Salt and freshly ground pepper

1. In a large saucepan, cook the lima beans according to the package directions; drain.

2. Wipe out the saucepan and heat the oil over medium heat until hot but not smoking. Add the onion, celery, and garlic and cook, stirring, for 3 minutes, or just until the onion begins to soften. Add the lima beans, tomato, corn, parsley, vinegar, 1/2 teaspoon salt, and 1/4 teaspoon pepper and cook, stirring, for 2 minutes, or until heated through.

3. Transfer to a bowl and serve warm, at room temperature, or chilled. **SERVES 4 TO 6**

santa fe *Salad*

this is an enticing salad that couldn't be simpler to prepare. Chop up a few vegetables and herbs, add a can of black beans, and toss with the robust southwestern-style dressing. Serve the salad on a bed of romaine lettuce, or roll up in warm flour tortillas together with grilled chicken strips and sour cream for a great lunch.

2 cups cooked black beans, drained and
   rinsed if canned
2 large plum tomatoes, seeded and cut
   into 1/4-inch dice
1/2 cup fresh, thawed frozen, or drained
   canned corn kernels

3 scallions, minced

1 jalapeño chile, seeded, ribs removed, and minced

2 tablespoons chopped fresh cilantro

1 small garlic clove, minced

2 tablespoons fruity olive oil

2 tablespoons fresh lime juice

Salt and ground red pepper

1. In a large bowl, combine the black beans, tomatoes, corn, scallions, jalapeño, cilantro, garlic, oil, lime juice, and salt and ground red pepper to taste. Toss until well mixed, spoon into a bowl, and serve.   **SERVES 4**

picnic Potato salad

this creamy, mayonnaise-dressed potato salad is the one you'll want to serve with fried chicken and cole slaw.

2 pounds red potatoes, cut into 1/2-inch cubes

1/2 cup each finely chopped celery

  and scallions

3 tablespoons vegetable oil

2 tablespoons white wine vinegar

2 teaspoons grainy mustard

Salt and freshly ground pepper

1/2 cup mayonnaise

2 hard-cooked large eggs,

  finely chopped

1/4 cup chopped fresh parsley

1. In a large pot, put the potatoes in salted water to cover and bring to a boil. Reduce the heat, cover, and simmer for 12 minutes, or until the potatoes are tender; drain.

2. In a large bowl, combine the hot potatoes, the celery, scallions, oil, vinegar, mustard, 1 teaspoon salt, and 1/4 teaspoon pepper; toss well. Cool to room temperature. Stir in the mayonnaise, eggs, and parsley and serve.

SERVES 6 TO 8

french Potato salad

the French are known for their potato salads. Here, a simple vinaigrette is tossed with warm, cooked potatoes. This special technique allows the dressing to be absorbed by the potatoes.

2 pounds waxy potatoes (about 6)

1/4 cup white vinegar

1 tablespoon Dijon mustard

1/4 cup plus 2 tablespoons olive oil

1/2 cup chopped scallions

1/3 cup chopped fresh parsley

Salt and freshly ground pepper

1. In a large pot, cover the potatoes with salted water, cover, and bring to a boil over high heat. Reduce the heat to low and simmer for about 30 minutes, or until the potatoes are tender; drain.

2. Meanwhile, in a large bowl, whisk together the vinegar and mustard until smooth. Add the oil in a slow stream, whisking until blended. Add the scallions and parsley and season with salt and pepper. Set aside.

3. When the potatoes are just cool enough to handle, slip off the skins and cut the still-warm potatoes into 1/2-inch chunks. Add to the dressing and gently toss until the potatoes absorb all the liquid. Serve warm or at room temperature.

SERVES 6

side dishes & salads

orzo & cherry *Tomato* salad

try using small pasta, such as orzo, in place of rice in grain salads—it's a welcome texture change. This zesty, full-flavored pasta salad is as delicious as it is colorful.

FRESH LEMON DRESSING

- 2 tablespoons extra-virgin olive oil
- 2 tablespoons fresh lemon juice
- 1 garlic clove, smashed with the flat side of a large knife
- 1/4 teaspoon dried thyme, crumbled
- Salt and freshly ground pepper

- 1 1/2 cups orzo
- 6 ounces green beans, cut into 1/4-inch pieces (about 1 cup)
- 2 cups small cherry tomatoes, halved
- 1/4 cup minced red onion
- 1/4 cup chopped fresh parsley

1. In a small bowl, whisk together the oil, lemon juice, garlic, thyme, 1/2 teaspoon salt, and 1/4 teaspoon pepper. Set aside.
2. Bring a large saucepan of salted water to a boil over high heat. Add the orzo and cook, stirring frequently, for 5 minutes. Stir in the green beans and cook for 4 to 6 minutes longer, until the orzo and beans are both tender. Drain and let cool to room temperature.

3. Transfer the orzo and green beans to a serving bowl. Add the cherry tomatoes, onion, and parsley. Remove the garlic clove from the dressing and discard. Whisk the dressing, pour over the salad, and toss until mixed. Season with salt and pepper if necessary and serve. **SERVES 6 TO 8**

Easter Dinner

melon chunks wrapped
in Prosciutto slices

Lemon-Parmesan Wafers
page 11

Tapenade Pinwheels
page 17

Cream of Celery Soup

Herb-Grilled Leg of Lamb
page 58

Roasted Asparagus with
Lemon and Pine Nuts
page 84

Orzo and Cherry Tomato Salad

dinner rolls

Strawberry
and Lemon Curd Tart
page 125

cranberry & wild Rice salad

this jewellike salad makes a fabulous presentation on a holiday buffet table, especially with smoked turkey or maple-glazed ham. While the rice is cooking, toast the pecans, chop the celery and scallions, and set out the dressing ingredients.

1 (14 1/2-ounce) can chicken broth

8 ounces wild rice (1 1/3 cups),
   rinsed and picked over

3 tablespoons extra-virgin olive oil

2 tablespoons white wine vinegar

Salt and freshly ground pepper

3/4 cup pecans, toasted and coarsely chopped

3/4 cup dried cranberries

1/3 cup finely chopped celery

1/4 cup thinly sliced scallions

1. In a large saucepan, bring the broth and 3 cups water to a boil over high heat. Stir in a large pinch of salt and the wild rice and return to a boil. Reduce the heat to low and simmer, uncovered, for 1 to 1 1/2 hours, until the rice is tender. Drain and let cool.

2. In a serving bowl, whisk together the oil, vinegar, 1/2 teaspoon salt, and 1/2 teaspoon pepper. Add the rice, pecans, cranberries, celery, and scallions and toss until mixed. Season with salt and pepper if necessary and serve.

S E R V E S   4   T O   6

side dishes
& salads

Chapter Five

Desserts

desserts

best-ever Devil's food cake

devil's food cake is known for its moistness and its rich reddish-brown color, which it gets from the baking soda in the batter. Using cocoa instead of chocolate gives the cake an especially intense chocolate flavor.

1/2 cup unsweetened cocoa powder

1/2 cup boiling water

2 1/4 cups sifted all-purpose flour

1 1/2 teaspoons baking soda

1/4 teaspoon salt

2/3 cup vegetable shortening

1 3/4 cups sugar

1 teaspoon vanilla extract

2 large eggs

1 1/3 cups sour cream

1. Preheat the oven to 350°F. Grease and flour two 9-inch round cake pans.

2. In a small bowl, whisk together the cocoa and boiling water until smooth. In a medium bowl, whisk together the flour, baking soda, and salt.

3. In a large bowl, beat the shortening, sugar, and vanilla with an electric mixer until "sandy" textured. Add the eggs one at a time, beating well after each addition. On low speed, beat in the flour mixture alternately with the sour cream, beginning and ending with the flour. Add the cocoa mixture and blend well. Divide the batter between the prepared pans.

4. Bake for 40 minutes, or until a toothpick inserted near the center comes out clean. Place the pans on wire racks and let cool for 20 minutes. Invert the layers onto the racks, then turn them right side up and let the cake layers cool completely.

5. Place one cake layer on a serving plate. Spread with about 1 cup of the Chocolate Frosting. Top with the remaining cake layer and spread the remaining frosting over the top and sides of the cake. **SERVES 10 TO 12**

CHOCOLATE FROSTING

6 ounces semisweet chocolate, chopped

2 tablespoons water

1/2 cup sugar

4 large egg yolks

3/4 teaspoon vanilla extract

1 cup (2 sticks) unsalted butter, cut into small pieces, at room temperature

1. In a double boiler set over simmering water, melt the chocolate with the water, whisking until smooth. Transfer to a large bowl.

2. In the cleaned double boiler set over simmering water, mix the sugar and egg yolks and heat, whisking constantly, for 3 to 5 minutes, until the sugar is dissolved and the mixture is pale and thick. Stir into the melted chocolate, then add the vanilla.

3. With an electric mixer, beat the frosting on high speed for 3 minutes, or until cooled to room temperature. Beat in the butter, one piece at a time, beating until smooth after each addition until well mixed.

chocolate Pan cake

t his is the ideal cake to take on a picnic because it's served right out of the pan. (If the weather is warm, however, be sure to keep the cake in a cool place.) The no-fuss frosting calls for only three ingredients and takes just minutes to put together. Coarsely grated chocolate makes a pretty topping sprinkled over the cake, but you can use whatever you have on hand: chopped pecans or walnuts, chocolate sprinkles, or even toasted coconut.

1 1/2 cups all-purpose flour

1 cup Dutch-process cocoa powder,

   sifted

1 tablespoon instant espresso powder

2 1/2 teaspoons baking powder

1/2 teaspoon baking soda

1/2 teaspoon salt

3/4 cup (1 1/2 sticks) unsalted butter,

   at room temperature

1 cup granulated sugar

3/4 cup packed brown sugar

3 large eggs

2 large egg yolks

2 teaspoons vanilla extract

1 1/2 cups buttermilk

FROSTING

1 cup sour cream, at room temperature

1 tablespoon heavy cream

5 ounces semisweet chocolate,

   melted and cooled until just warm

1/2 ounce semisweet chocolate,

   coarsely grated

1. Preheat the oven to 350°F. Butter a 13- x 9-inch baking pan.

2. In a medium bowl, whisk together the flour, cocoa, espresso powder, baking powder, baking soda, and salt.

3. In a large bowl, beat the butter with an electric mixer until creamy. Gradually add the granulated and brown sugars and beat until light and fluffy. Beat in the eggs and egg yolks one at a time, beating well after each addition. Beat in the vanilla. On low speed, add the flour mixture alternately with the buttermilk in two or three additions, beginning and ending with the flour mixture. Spoon the batter into the prepared pan and smooth the top with a rubber spatula.

4. Bake for 35 minutes, or until the cake is springy to the touch. (The cake may sink slightly in the middle.) Put the pan on a wire rack and let the cake cool completely in the pan.

5. Make the frosting. In a medium bowl, gently but thoroughly stir the sour cream and heavy cream into the cooled chocolate until thoroughly blended. With a rubber spatula, spread over the top of the cake. Sprinkle the grated chocolate on top and refrigerate the cake until ready to serve.

SERVES 10 TO 12

desserts

pineapple Upside-down cake

 ust one slice of this cake will remind you why you loved this fruity syrupy treat as a child. The enticing flavors of cinnamon, nutmeg, and ginger lend this version a sophisticated accent. Serve it warm from the oven with softened vanilla ice cream.

1/2 cup (1 stick) unsalted butter

1/2 cup packed dark brown sugar

8 slices canned pineapple (from a
  20-ounce can)

1 1/4 cups all-purpose flour

3/4 cup granulated sugar

2 teaspoons baking powder

1/4 teaspoon ground cinnamon

1/4 teaspoon grated nutmeg

1/4 teaspoon ground ginger

1/4 teaspoon salt

Very small pinch freshly ground pepper

1/2 cup milk

1 large egg

1 1/2 teaspoons vanilla extract

1. Preheat the oven to 350°F.

2. In a small saucepan, melt 1/4 cup of the butter over low heat. Remove from the heat and stir in the brown sugar until well mixed. With a rubber spatula, spread the butter-sugar mixture evenly over the bottom of a 9-inch round cake pan. Place one of the pineapple rings in the center of the pan on top of the butter-sugar mixture. Arrange the remaining pineapple slices in a circle around the center pineapple slice. Set the pan aside.

3. In a large bowl, whisk together the flour, granulated sugar, baking powder, cinnamon, nutmeg, ginger, salt, and pepper.

4. In a small saucepan, melt the remaining 1/4 cup butter. Pour the milk into a small bowl. Add the melted butter, egg, and vanilla and whisk with a fork until blended. Pour the milk mixture over the flour mixture and stir until just combined. Scrape the batter over the pineapple rings and gently smooth the top with a rubber spatula.

5. Bake for 30 to 35 minutes, until golden brown and a toothpick inserted into the center comes out clean.

6. Let the cake cool in the pan on a wire rack for 5 minutes. Invert the cake onto a serving plate and let stand for about 1 minute before lifting off the pan. Serve warm or at room temperature. **SERVES 6 TO 8**

fresh lemon Pound cake

a springtime baby or bridal shower is the ideal occasion for serving this fine-textured lemony cake. Surround the cake with a garland of raspberries, blueberries, and blackberries, and tuck in little sprigs of fresh mint. Heavy cream that is sweetened, whipped to billowy peaks, and served in a cut-glass bowl completes the moment.

3 1/2 cups sifted cake flour (not self-rising)

1/2 teaspoon baking powder

1/4 teaspoon salt

1 cup (2 sticks) unsalted butter, at room temperature

1/2 cup vegetable shortening

1 1/2 cups sugar

6 large eggs

1 scant cup milk

1 tablespoon grated lemon zest (from about 2 lemons)

1 teaspoon vanilla extract

1 teaspoon lemon extract

Confectioners' sugar, for serving

1. Place an oven rack in the middle of the oven and preheat the oven to 300°F. Grease and flour a 10-inch Bundt pan.

2. In a medium bowl, whisk together the flour, baking powder, and salt.

3. In a large bowl, cream the butter and shortening with an electric mixer. Gradually add the sugar, beating until light and fluffy. Beat in the eggs one at a time, beating well after each addition. On low speed, add the flour mixture alternately with the milk, beginning and ending with the flour mixture. Stir in the lemon zest, vanilla extract, and lemon extract. Scrape the batter into the prepared pan and smooth the top.

4. Bake for 1 1/2 hours, or until a toothpick inserted into the center comes out clean. Let the cake cool in the pan on a wire rack for 10 minutes, then invert the cake onto the rack and let cool completely.

5. Just before serving, dust the cake with confectioners' sugar.

SERVES 10 TO 12

Bridal Shower

Mixed Greens
Honey Mustard Dressing
page 100

Lemon & Chive Salmon Cakes
page 73

Tarragon Tartar Sauce
page 73

Angel Biscuits

Confetti Cole Slaw
page 105

Fresh Lemon Pound Cake

apple cider Gingerbread

ingerbread may be the world's best cold-weather dessert, and baking doesn't get simpler than this. The cake is mixed and baked in the same pan, so your kids will be perfect helpers here. Keep in mind that gingerbread tastes best when it's fresh from the oven—put it in to bake when you sit down to dinner, and you will have fragrant, moist gingerbread just in time for dessert.

- 1 1/2 cups all-purpose flour
- 1/2 cup packed dark brown sugar
- 1 teaspoon ground ginger
- 1 teaspoon baking soda
- 1/2 cup apple cider or apple juice
- 1/3 cup vegetable oil
- 1/4 cup molasses
- 1 tablespoon cider vinegar
- 1 tablespoon minced crystallized ginger

LEMON SAUCE

- 1 cup sour cream or plain yogurt
- Grated zest of 1 lemon
- 2 teaspoons fresh lemon juice
- 1/4 teaspoon vanilla extract

1. Preheat the oven to 350°F.

2. Into an 8-inch round cake pan, sift together the flour, brown sugar, ground ginger, and baking soda. Make a well in the center of the flour mixture and add the apple cider, oil, molasses, vinegar, and crystallized ginger. With a fork, stir just until the batter is smooth.

3. Bake for 30 to 35 minutes, until a toothpick inserted in the center comes out clean. Transfer the cake to a wire rack.

4. Meanwhile, in a small bowl, stir together the sour cream, lemon zest, lemon juice, and vanilla. Refrigerate.

5. Cut the warm gingerbread into wedges and serve accompanied by the lemon sauce. **SERVES 8**

cranberry-tangerine Cheesecake

GRAHAM CRACKER CRUST

1 1/4 cups graham cracker crumbs

1 tablespoon sugar

1/2 teaspoon ground cinnamon

1/4 cup (1/2 stick) unsalted butter, melted

CHEESE FILLING

1 envelope unflavored gelatin

1/4 cup cold water

2 (8-ounce) packages cream cheese,
   at room temperature

3 large eggs, separated and at room
   temperature (see Note)

3/4 cup sugar

1 teaspoon grated tangerine zest

1/2 cup fresh tangerine juice

2 tablespoons fresh lemon juice

1 teaspoon vanilla extract

1 cup sour cream, at room temperature

CRANBERRY TOPPING

1/2 cup fresh tangerine juice

3/4 cup sugar

2 cups fresh cranberries

2 tablespoons water blended with
   1 tablespoon cornstarch

1. Preheat the oven to 375°F.

2. In a medium bowl, mix the graham cracker crumbs, sugar, and cinnamon. Stir in the melted butter until blended, then press over the bottom of a 9-inch springform pan. Bake for 8 to 10 minutes, until golden. Let cool on a wire rack.

3. In a small saucepan, sprinkle the gelatin over the cold water. Let stand for 5 minutes.

4. Meanwhile, in a large bowl, beat the cream cheese, egg yolks, and sugar with an electric mixer until light and fluffy.

5. Heat the gelatin mixture over low heat, stirring, until the gelatin is dissolved. Gradually beat the gelatin, tangerine zest and juice, lemon juice, and vanilla into the cheese mixture.

6. In a medium bowl, beat the egg whites with an electric mixer until soft peaks begin to form. Fold the sour cream into the cream cheese mixture, then fold in the egg whites. Pour the mixture into the pan. Cover with plastic wrap, pressing it onto the surface, and refrigerate for at least 4 hours, or overnight.

7. In a medium saucepan, bring the tangerine juice and sugar to a boil and boil for 2 minutes. Add the cranberries, bring to a simmer, and cook for 1 minute. Stir the cornstarch mixture into the cranberry mixture and bring to a boil, stirring constantly. Reduce the heat and simmer for 1 minute. Cool completely, then cover and refrigerate until ready to serve.

8. To serve, run a knife around the edge of the cheesecake and release the pan sides. Spread the topping over the cheesecake; serve. Refrigerate any leftovers. **SERVES 10**

Note: Pregnant women, the very young, elderly, or anyone with a compromised immune system should not eat raw eggs.

zucchini-lemon Quick bread

q uick bread, aptly named since it doesn't require kneading or rising time, is a great casual snack. It's perfect for eating out of hand, or for wrapping in waxed paper and packing with a take-along lunch. In this version, the combination of zucchini, cranberries, almonds, and lemon zest is unbeatable. This recipe is a great way to use up an overabundance of zucchini at summer's end. As with all quick breads, the flavor improves when it is wrapped in plastic and allowed to stand overnight at room temperature. Spread with a little cream cheese and served with a cup of tea, this cake makes a welcome mid-afternoon snack.

desserts

1 1/2 cups all-purpose flour

2 teaspoons baking powder

1/2 teaspoon baking soda

1 teaspoon ground cinnamon

1/4 teaspoon ground allspice

1/4 teaspoon grated nutmeg

1/4 teaspoon salt

3/4 cup sugar

6 tablespoons unsalted butter, melted
   and cooled

2 large eggs

2 tablespoons grated lemon zest

1/4 cup fresh lemon juice (about
   1 large lemon)

1 teaspoon vanilla extract

2 cups grated zucchini

1 cup finely chopped blanched almonds
   (about 3 1/2 ounces)

1/2 cup dried cranberries or
   golden raisins

1. Preheat the oven to 350°F. Grease a 9- x 5-inch loaf pan.

2. In a medium bowl, whisk together the flour, baking powder, baking soda, cinnamon, allspice, nutmeg, and salt.

3. In a large bowl, beat the sugar, melted butter, eggs, lemon zest and juice, and vanilla with an electric mixer until well blended. With a rubber spatula or a wooden spoon, stir in the zucchini. Add the flour mixture and stir until blended. Fold in the almonds and cranberries. Scrape the batter into the prepared pan, smoothing the top with a rubber spatula.

4. Bake for about 1 hour, or until a toothpick inserted into the center comes out clean. Let the quick bread cool in the pan for 10 minutes, then turn out onto a wire rack and let cool completely. Cut into 1/2-inch slices and serve.

SERVES 10 TO 12

deep-dish
Apple-cranberry pie

deep-dish pies are scrumptious, homey desserts, meant to be topped with generous scoops of ice cream. The cranberry, apple, and nut filling will remind you of a rich fruit conserve put up for the long winter ahead.

FLAKY CRUST

1 cup all-purpose flour

1/4 teaspoon salt

3 tablespoons cold unsalted butter, cut into pieces

2 tablespoons vegetable shortening,

   chilled and cut into pieces

3 to 4 tablespoons ice water

FRUIT FILLING

2 pounds tart apples, such as Empire or

   Granny Smith, peeled, quartered, cored,

   and cut into 1/4-inch slices (about 7 cups)

1/3 cup all-purpose flour

1 cup fresh cranberries

3/4 cup sugar

1/2 cup golden raisins

1/2 cup chopped pecans

1/4 cup dried cranberries (optional)

1 large egg beaten with 1 teaspoon

   water, for brushing

Sugar, for sprinkling

1. In a food processor, combine the flour and salt and pulse until blended. Distribute the butter and vegetable shortening on top of the flour and pulse until the mixture resembles coarse meal. Add the water 1 tablespoon at a time, pulsing just until a soft crumbly dough forms. Shape the dough into a disk, wrap in plastic, and refrigerate for at least 1 hour, or overnight.

2. Preheat the oven to 375°F.

3. Make the fruit filling. In a large bowl, toss together the apples and flour until the apples are evenly coated with flour.

4. In a food processor, combine the fresh cranberries and sugar and pulse until the cranberries are coarsely chopped. Add to the apple mixture along with the raisins, pecans, and dried cranberries, if using, and toss until mixed. Spoon the filling into a 9 1/2-inch deep-dish pie plate.

5. On a lightly floured surface, roll out the dough to an 11-inch round. Brush the edge of the pie plate with water and drape the dough over the fruit. Trim the dough to a 3/4-inch overhang and fold under. Press the dough against the moistened edge of the pie plate and crimp. With a small knife, cut several steam vents in the crust. Brush the dough with the beaten egg and sprinkle lightly with sugar.

6. Set the pie plate on a baking sheet to catch any drips. Bake for about 1 hour, or until the crust is nicely browned, the filling is bubbly, and the apples are tender. Let the pie cool on a wire rack. Serve warm or at room temperature.

SERVES 8

apple-cinnamon Crumb pie

S coop some leftover pie into a bowl of your favorite cereal brand and top with a generous dollop of plain or vanilla-flavored yogurt for a breakfast treat.

FLAKY CRUST

1 cup all-purpose flour

1/4 teaspoon salt

3 tablespoons cold unsalted butter,
   cut into pieces

2 tablespoons vegetable shortening,
   chilled and cut into pieces

3 to 4 tablespoons cold water

WALNUT-CRUMB TOPPING

1/3 cup walnuts

1/3 cup all-purpose flour

1/3 cup packed dark brown sugar

1/4 teaspoon ground cinnamon

Pinch of salt

3 tablespoons cold unsalted butter,
   cut into pieces

APPLE FILLING

2 1/2 pounds tart apples, such as
   Granny Smith, peeled, quartered,
   cored, and cut into 1/2-inch slices

2 tablespoons fresh lemon juice

1/2 cup granulated sugar

2 tablespoons all-purpose flour

1/2 teaspoon ground cinnamon

1. In a food processor, combine the flour and salt and pulse until blended. Distribute the butter and vegetable shortening on top of the flour and pulse until the mixture resembles coarse crumbs. Add the water one tablespoon at a time and pulse just until a soft, crumbly dough forms. Shape the dough into a disk, wrap in plastic, and refrigerate for at least 1 hour, or overnight.

2. Preheat the oven to 375°F.

3. On a lightly floured surface, roll out the dough to an 11-inch round. Carefully fit the dough into a 9-inch pie plate. Trim and crimp the edges. Refrigerate.

4. Make the walnut-crumb topping. In a food processor, coarsely chop the walnuts. Transfer to a medium bowl. Add the flour, brown sugar, cinnamon, and salt to the processor and pulse until mixed. Add the butter and pulse until the mixture is crumbly. Add to the walnuts and mix until the topping resembles coarse crumbs. Set aside.

5. Make the apple filling. In a large bowl, toss the apples with the lemon juice. Add the sugar, flour, and cinnamon and toss until well mixed. Spoon the apple filling into the pie shell and sprinkle the crumb topping over.

6. Place the pie plate on a baking sheet to catch any drips. Bake for 55 to 60 minutes, until the crust is browned and the apples are tender. Let the pie cool on a wire rack. Serve warm or at room temperature.   **SERVES 8**

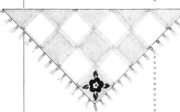

desserts

strawberry & lemon curd Tart

 fresh ripe strawberries—arranged on top of a thick, tangy lemon curd and a no-fuss sour cream crust— are an irresistible finishing touch to this warm-weather dessert. Prepare the crust and curd a day ahead and assemble the tart right before serving.

1/2 cup granulated sugar

5 tablespoons cold unsalted butter,
   cut into pieces

2 large eggs

2 tablespoons grated lemon zest

1/4 cup fresh lemon juice
   (from 1 large lemon)

SOUR CREAM CRUST

1 1/2 cups all-purpose flour

1/4 cup plus 2 tablespoons confectioners'
   sugar

1/2 cup (1 stick) cold unsalted butter,
   cut into small pieces

Pinch of salt

3 tablespoons sour cream

1 large egg yolk

1/4 teaspoon vanilla extract

1 1/2 pints small strawberries, hulled

1/4 cup heavy cream, whipped

1. In a double boiler or in a metal bowl set over a saucepan of simmering water, combine the granulated sugar, butter, eggs, and lemon zest and juice. Cook, whisking frequently, for 12 to 15 minutes, until the mixture is thick enough to hold the marks of the whisk and bubbles just begin to appear on the surface. Press the mixture through a strainer set over a medium bowl and let cool to room temperature. Cover with plastic wrap and refrigerate for at least 1 hour, or for up to several hours.

2. Make the sour cream crust. In a food processor, combine the flour, confectioners' sugar, butter, and salt and pulse until the mixture resembles coarse meal.

3. In a small bowl, stir together the sour cream, egg yolk, and vanilla until well combined. Spoon over the flour mixture and process until a ball of dough forms. Shape the dough into a disk, wrap in plastic, and refrigerate for at least 30 minutes, or until firm.

4. On a lightly floured surface, roll out the dough to an 11-inch round about 3/8 inch thick. With two pancake spatulas, transfer the dough to an ungreased baking sheet. Crimp the edges decoratively and refrigerate for 20 minutes.

5. Preheat the oven to 375°F.

6. With a fork, prick the dough all over. Bake for 15 to 17 minutes, until lightly golden. Let the pastry cool completely on the baking sheet set on a wire rack.

7. Spread the lemon filling evenly over the pastry, leaving a 1-inch border around the edge. Arrange the strawberries on top of the lemon filling. In a small bowl, whip the cream until stiff peaks form. Spoon the cream into a pastry bag fitted with a star tip and pipe rosettes between the strawberries. Transfer the tart to a platter and serve.   **S E R V E S   8   T O   1 0**

desserts

farmhouse
Walnut pie

Walnuts, less rich-tasting than pecans, make this variation on pecan pie a welcome change. Here, brown sugar and dark corn syrup give the pie a deep caramel flavor (if you prefer a subtler flavor, use light corn syrup instead).

FLAKY CRUST

1 cup all-purpose flour

1/4 teaspoon salt

3 tablespoons cold unsalted butter,

cut into pieces

2 tablespoons vegetable shortening,

well-chilled and cut into

small pieces

3 to 4 tablespoons ice water

WALNUT FILLING

1 3/4 cups walnuts

4 large eggs

3/4 cup packed light brown sugar

3/4 cup dark corn syrup

1/4 cup (1/2 stick) unsalted butter,

melted

1 tablespoon sour mash whiskey

(optional)

1 1/2 teaspoons vanilla extract

1/4 teaspoon salt

HONEY WHIPPED CREAM

1 cup heavy cream

3 tablespoons honey

1. In a food processor, combine the flour and salt and process until blended. Distribute the butter and vegetable shortening over the top of the flour and pulse until the mixture resembles coarse meal. Add the water one tablespoon at time and pulse just until a soft crumbly dough forms. Shape the dough into a disk, wrap in plastic, and refrigerate for 1 hour, or overnight.

2. On a lightly floured surface, roll out the dough to an 11-inch round. Fit into a 9-inch pie plate. Trim and crimp the edges. Refrigerate.

3. Preheat the oven to 375°F.

4. Make the walnut filling. Spread the walnuts in a baking pan and toast, tossing occasionally, for about 15 minutes, or until lightly golden. Transfer to a plate and let cool.

5. In a large bowl, whisk together the eggs and brown sugar until smooth. Add the corn syrup, butter, whiskey, if using, the vanilla, and salt and whisk until smooth. Stir in the walnuts and pour into the pie shell.

6. Bake for 35 to 40 minutes, until the filling is puffed and firm in the center and the crust is lightly browned. Let the pie cool to room temperature on a wire rack.

7. In a medium bowl, beat the cream and honey with an electric mixer until stiff peaks begin to form. Transfer to a serving bowl.

8. Serve the pie accompanied by the cream. Refrigerate any leftovers. **SERVES 8**

brown sugar
Pumpkin pie

I t just wouldn't be Thanksgiving without a rich, custardy pumpkin pie gracing the table. And this spectacular version—sweetened with the warm flavor of brown sugar, accented with cinnamon, nutmeg, and ginger, and served with maple-scented whipped cream—is bound to become a standard on your holiday menu.

desserts

FLAKY CRUST

1 cup all-purpose flour

1/4 teaspoon salt

3 tablespoons cold unsalted butter, cut into pieces

2 tablespoons vegetable shortening, chilled and
   cut into pieces

3 to 4 tablespoons cold water

PUMPKIN FILLING

2/3 cup packed light brown sugar

3 large eggs

2 tablespoons molasses

1 teaspoon ground cinnamon

3/4 teaspoon grated nutmeg

1/2 teaspoon ground ginger

1/8 teaspoon salt

1 (16-ounce) can solid-pack pumpkin

1 1/4 cups light cream or half-and-half

1 teaspoon vanilla extract

MAPLE WHIPPED CREAM

1 cup heavy cream

1 tablespoon maple syrup

1 tablespoon light brown sugar

1. In a food processor, combine the flour and salt and process until blended. Distribute the butter and vegetable shortening on top of the flour and pulse until the mixture resembles coarse meal. Add the water one tablespoon at a time and pulse until a crumbly dough forms. Shape the dough into a disk. Wrap in plastic and refrigerate for at least 1 hour, or overnight.

2. On a lightly floured surface, roll out the dough to a 12-inch round. Carefully fit the dough into a 9-inch pie plate. Trim and crimp the dough to form a high fluted edge. Refrigerate.

3. Preheat the oven to 425°F.

4. In a large bowl, whisk the brown sugar, eggs, molasses, cinnamon, nutmeg, ginger, and salt until well blended. Whisk in the pumpkin, then add the cream and vanilla, whisking until smooth. Pour into the prepared pie shell.

5. Bake for 15 minutes. Reduce the oven temperature to 325°F. Bake for 35 to 40 minutes longer, until the filling is puffed and set around the edges but not in the very center. Let the pie cool on a wire rack.

6. In a medium bowl, beat the cream, maple syrup, and brown sugar with an electric mixer until stiff peaks form. Spoon into a serving bowl.

7. Serve the pie accompanied by the whipped cream. Refrigerate any leftovers. **SERVES 8**

desserts

fresh nectarine & blueberry *Cobbler*

 obblers—baked treats made of sweetened fruit topped with biscuits—are great, flexible desserts. If you like, substitute peaches or apricots for the nectarines and raspberries or blackberries for the blueberries to get equally splendid results. Although it's not traditional, you can add a generous pinch of ground ginger, cinnamon, or nutmeg to the fruit for a flavorful variation. But, please, don't change the biscuits! They're delectable just the way they are.

8 small ripe nectarines, pitted and

cut into 1/4-inch wedges

(about 4 1/2 cups)

1 pint blueberries

1/2 cup sugar, or to taste

1 tablespoon plus 1 teaspoon cornstarch

1/2 cup water

1 tablespoon fresh lemon juice

BISCUIT TOPPING

1 3/4 cups all-purpose flour, sifted

3 tablespoons sugar

1 tablespoon baking powder

Pinch of salt

1 cup heavy cream

Milk, for brushing

Sugar, for sprinkling

Vanilla ice cream, for serving

(optional)

1. Preheat the oven to 450°F.

2. In a large saucepan, combine the nectarines, blueberries, sugar, cornstarch, water, and lemon juice. Bring the mixture to a boil, stirring constantly. Reduce the heat and simmer for 5 minutes, or until the fruit has softened. Transfer the mixture to a shallow 1 1/2-quart baking dish. Set aside.

3. Make the biscuit topping. Into a large bowl, sift together the flour, sugar, baking powder, and salt. Make a well in the center.

4. In a medium bowl, whip the cream just until soft peaks form. Spoon the cream into the well and mix with a fork just until a dough forms.

5. On a lightly floured surface, gently knead the dough several times. Roll or pat the dough out until 3/4 inch thick. With a 2 1/2-inch round biscuit cutter, cut out 6 biscuits. Arrange the biscuits on top of the fruit mixture, brush them with milk, and sprinkle the biscuits with sugar.

6. Bake the cobbler for 15 to 17 minutes, until the biscuits are browned and the fruit is bubbling. Let cool slightly, then serve warm with ice cream, if desired. **SERVES 6**

caramel Baked pears

Serve this easy dessert on a Sunday night: it tastes special, but doesn't take much time to prepare. Bake the pears in the morning, transfer them to a clean baking dish, and refrigerate. Chill the caramel sauce in a separate container. To serve, reheat the pears, covered, in a 350°F oven, and gently warm the sauce in the microwave or over very low heat. Just be sure to use pears that are ripe and sweet for the best flavor.

3 tablespoons unsalted butter

4 medium firm-ripe pears (about 2 pounds)

1/4 cup plus 2 tablespoons sugar

1/3 cup heavy cream

1. Preheat the oven to 400°F.

2. Put the butter into a shallow baking dish just large enough to hold the pears in a single layer and place in the oven until the butter melts.

3. Meanwhile, peel the pears and cut in half. Remove the cores with a melon baller or small knife and cut out the blossom ends.

4. Place the pears in the baking dish and gently turn them in the butter until well coated, leaving them cut-side down. Bake for 10 minutes. Sprinkle the pears with the sugar. Using two rubber spatulas, turn the pears in the butter-sugar mixture, leaving the pears cut-side down.

5. Bake for 40 to 50 minutes longer, basting the pears often with the pan juices, until they are very tender and the pan juices are bubbly and light caramel in color. Using a slotted spoon, transfer the pears to individual dessert plates or to a platter.

6. Pour the cream into the hot baking dish. Using a rubber spatula, scrape down the pan sides and stir until the pan juices and cream are well mixed. If necessary, briefly return the pan to the oven to dissolve any bits of caramel.

7. To serve, spoon the sauce over the pears, or pour into a small pitcher and pass separately.

SERVES 4 TO 6

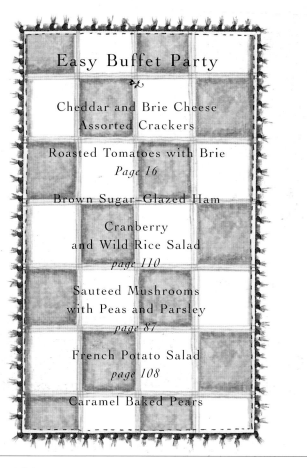

Easy Buffet Party

Cheddar and Brie Cheese
Assorted Crackers

Roasted Tomatoes with Brie
Page 16

Brown Sugar–Glazed Ham

Cranberry
and Wild Rice Salad
page 110

Sauteed Mushrooms
with Peas and Parsley
page 87

French Potato Salad
page 108

Caramel Baked Pears

double pear Crisp

C hoosing the right variety of pear for this mouth-watering dessert is easy—any large pear, such as Bartlett, Bosc, or Anjou will do. Knowing how to pick pears is a little trickier. Look for fruit that is firm (not rock hard) and without bruises. Often pears are sold when they are still unripe and very hard. It may take several days for them to ripen until they are soft but not mushy, but it's well worth the wait. Bartletts go from green to pale yellow when ripe, Boscs go from greenish-brown to milk-chocolate brown, and Anjous yield slightly when gently pressed. When your pears are ripe, refrigerate until ready to use. Dried pears, which intensify the pear flavor here, are available in many supermarkets and in specialty food stores.

desserts

2 tablespoons granulated sugar

1/8 teaspoon grated nutmeg

5 medium firm-ripe pears (about 2 1/4
    pounds), peeled, halved, cored,
    and cut into 1/2-inch chunks

4 ounces dried pears (about 5 large halves),
    snipped or cut into 3/4-inch pieces

1 tablespoon amaretto or brandy

ALMOND-CRUMB TOPPING

1/2 cup all-purpose flour

1/2 cup packed light brown sugar

Pinch of salt

1/4 cup (1/2 stick) unsalted butter,
    cut into pieces

1/2 cup sliced natural almonds

1. Preheat the oven to 375°F.

2. Combine the sugar and nutmeg in a 9-inch square baking dish. Add the fresh and dried pears and sprinkle with the amaretto, tossing until the pears are evenly coated with the sugar. Set aside.

3. Make the almond-crumb topping. In a food processor, combine the flour, brown sugar, and salt and pulse until blended. Distribute the butter evenly over the flour mixture and pulse until the mixture is crumbly. Add the almonds and pulse just until mixed.

4. Sprinkle the crumb topping over the pears. Bake for 40 to 50 minutes, until the fresh pears are tender when pierced with a small knife and the topping is crisp and browned.

SERVES 4 TO 6

peanut brittle fudge Sundae

t his dessert is a runaway favorite with kids. To chop the peanut brittle easily, put it into a zip-top freezer bag and crush coarsely with a mallet or rolling pin. When the peanut brittle is heated, it forms a silky sauce with great crunchy bits. For even more peanut flavor, sprinkle the sundae with chopped unsalted peanuts or coarsely chopped Heath bars.

6 ounces bittersweet or semisweet chocolate,
   coarsely chopped
2 tablespoons unsalted butter
1 cup heavy cream
3/4 cup coarsely crushed peanut brittle
1 to 2 pints premium-quality vanilla
   ice cream, for serving

1. In a heavy medium saucepan, heat the chocolate, butter, and cream over low heat, stirring until the chocolate and butter are melted and the sauce is smooth. Remove from the heat and set aside until just warm.
2. Stir the peanut brittle into the chocolate sauce.
3. Scoop the ice cream into dessert dishes and top with the sauce. Serve immediately.

S E R V E S   4   O R   5

Children's
Birthday Party

Potato Chips

Popcorn

Baked Double Cheese
and Macaroni
page 88

Mini Burgers on Buns

Iceberg Lettuce Wedges
Carrot Sticks
Honey Mustard Dressing
page 100

Peanut Brittle Fudge Sundaes

Chocolate Pan Cake
page 114

triple-berry Summer pudding

desserts

this is the queen of make-ahead desserts. In fact, it is absolutely essential that it be prepared ahead of time so the pudding has a chance to set up. A summer pudding is an ambrosial amalgam of sliced white bread and ripe, juicy berries layered in a bowl. Feel free to change the proportion of berries here, especially if you happen to have a blackberry patch in your backyard. Serve with softly whipped cream or rich vanilla ice cream.

2 pints blueberries

1/4 cup plus 2 tablespoons sugar

1/2 teaspoon vanilla extract

1 cup raspberries

1 cup sliced strawberries

2 tablespoons or more unsalted butter,
     at room temperature

About 12 slices firm-textured white bread,
     crusts removed

Blueberries, raspberries, and fresh mint sprigs,
     for garnish

Fresh mint sprigs

Sweetened whipped cream, for serving

1. In a large saucepan, combine the blueberries and 1/4 cup of the sugar and cook over medium heat until the berries begin to release their juices. Increase the heat to medium-high and bring to a boil. Boil gently, stirring frequently, for 10 minutes, or until the juices thicken. Remove from the heat and add the vanilla.

2. In a medium bowl, stir together the raspberries, strawberries, and the remaining 2 tablespoons sugar, crushing the berries slightly with the back of a spoon.

3. Line a 6-cup bowl with plastic wrap, leaving a 6-inch overhang all around. Lightly butter one side of each slice of bread. Line the bowl with the bread slices, buttered side down, cutting the bread to fit as necessary. Spoon the raspberry mixture into the bowl and smooth the top. Top with a layer of bread, cutting the bread to fit. Spoon the blueberry mixture over then cover with another layer of bread, cutting the bread to fit.

4. Fold the plastic over the pudding and top with a plate slightly smaller than the bowl. Weight with a 1-pound can and refrigerate for at least 10 or for up to 24 hours.

5. To serve, invert the pudding onto a serving plate and carefully remove the bowl and plastic wrap. Serve the pudding garnished with blueberries, raspberries, and mint sprigs. Pass the whipped cream separately. **SERVES 8**

lemony plum Compote

desserts

italian prune plums, the variety to use here, can be found in produce markets beginning in late August. These free-stone, bluish-purple plums are always reasonably priced and are good for eating. Stewed or baked, however, their rich intoxicating flavor really shines through. This compote, very simple and very delicious, shows just how luscious these plums can be.

I 1/2 pounds ripe Italian prune plums,
   pitted and quartered

1/4 cup sugar or to taste (depending on
   the sweetness of the plums)

1/4 cup prune juice

2 tablespoons brandy or vodka

Zest of 1 lemon (removed in strips with
   a vegetable peeler)

I 1/2 pints vanilla ice cream

1. In a serving bowl, combine the plums, sugar, prune juice, brandy, and lemon zest. Cover with plastic wrap and let stand at room temperature for about 3 hours, stirring occasionally. Discard the lemon zest.

2. Scoop the ice cream into individual bowls, top with the plum compote, and serve. **SERVES 6**

creamy apricot Sorbet

Y ou just can't beat a one-ingredient dessert for simplicity. Not only is this sorbet incredibly easy to prepare, but it is also full of the lush perfumed flavor of tree-ripened apricots. Serve in small scoops with an assortment of seasonal berries, or spoon a little fresh raspberry or strawberry sauce into the dish before scooping. And if you have lemon balm, mint, or lemon verbena growing in your garden, use some for a lovely, sweetly scented garnish.

2 (15-ounce) cans apricot halves

in heavy syrup

1. Drain one can of fruit. Put the drained fruit and the remaining fruit, with its syrup, in a large heavy-duty zip-top plastic bag. Freeze for 6 hours, or until just frozen, but still a bit slushy.

2. Spoon the mixture into a food processor and process until smooth. Transfer the sorbet to a metal pan, cover with foil, and freeze for at least 1 hour.

3. Let the sorbet stand at room temperature for about 15 minutes, or until soft enough to scoop, then serve.

S E R V E S   4

Dessert Party

Blueberry Sorbet
with Melon Ribbons
page 141

Creamy Apricot Sorbet

Fresh Lemon Pound Cake
page 117

Seasonal berries

Best-Ever
Devil's Food Cake
page 115

Apple Cider Gingerbread
page 119

Shortbread cookies

Warm chocolate chip cookies

blueberry sorbet with melon Ribbons

intensely flavored, deeply colored blueberry sorbet is an eye-catching contrast next to ribbons of pale green honeydew. Try cantaloupe for a flavorful alternative, or use a combination if you have both on hand. And if you have an ice cream maker, don't hesitate to use it here. For a change of pace, instead of scooping the sorbet, turn it into a granita, sorbet Italian style, by using a metal spoon to scrape shards of the sorbet into serving bowls or extra-large wine goblets.

and freeze for at least 1 hour, or until firm enough to scoop.

4. With a vegetable peeler, cut about 3 cups very long wide strips from the honeydew and arrange decoratively in individual bowls or on dessert plates. Place a scoop of the sorbet on the melon ribbons, garnish with raspberries, if using, and serve. **SERVES 6**

**1 pint fresh blueberries, picked over and
   rinsed or thawed frozen blueberries**

1/2 cup sugar

1 1/4 cups water

1 tablespoon fresh lemon juice

**1/4 large ripe honeydew melon, peeled
   and seeded**

Raspberries, for garnish (optional)

1. In a food processor or a blender, combine the blueberries, sugar, water, and lemon juice. Process until pureed, then pour through a coarse strainer set over a large bowl. Press firmly on the solids with the back of a wooden spoon to extract as much of the liquid as possible. Discard the solids.

2. Pour the mixture into an 8-inch square baking pan and freeze for 6 hours, or until just frozen, but still a bit slushy.

3. Spoon the blueberry mixture into a food processor and process until smooth. Transfer to a metal pan, cover with foil.

very chocolate Pudding

So rich and creamy, this very chocolatey pudding tastes like it was made from scratch. Dress it up with a swirl of whipped cream and a sprinkling of cinnamon, cocoa, or both. If you prefer your chocolate pudding without a skin on top, press a piece of plastic wrap directly onto the surface of the pudding before chilling.

2 (3.4-ounce) packages chocolate pudding mix (not instant)

2 cups half-and-half

2 cups milk

1 (6-ounce) package semisweet chocolate chips (1 cup)

2 to 3 tablespoons dark rum, amaretto, or brandy (optional)

1 teaspoon vanilla extract

1. Put the pudding mix into a large saucepan. Whisk in the half-and-half and milk and continue whisking until the pudding is smooth. Place the pan over medium heat and bring to a boil, stirring constantly with a wooden spoon. Remove the pan from the heat.

2. Add the chocolate chips and stir until melted and smooth. Stir in the rum, if using, and the vanilla. Spoon the pudding into a serving dish or individual dessert dishes. Refrigerate until ready to serve. **SERVES 6 TO 8**

desserts

Index